THE JOB SEARCH BIBLE

EARLY CAREERS EDITION

MATT SEDGWICK

HUW LANDAUER

First Published 2021

Copyright ©2021 Matt Sedgwick, Huw Landauer

This book is a revised edition of The Let's Role Job Search
Bible, first published in 2020.

ISBN: 9798463630223

CONTENTS

INTRODUCTION

If you're reading this book, you belong to one of four groups of people:

1. You're early in your career and looking for a job.
2. You already have a job, but you want to keep your set of jobseeking tools sharp.
3. You're a recruiter, hiring manager or copywriter checking over our advice, hoping to catch us out.
4. You're stranded on a desert island and have resorted to reading this book to stave off the ever-advancing madness caused by prolonged social isolation.

It should come as no surprise that we have written this book for groups 1 and 2 (though group 4 have our deepest sympathies). We wanted to write it because, as an experienced recruiter and a recent graduate, the two of us have a good idea of what it feels like to float around the job market, and what it takes to paddle yourself in the right direction. We thought we'd write it all down in a way that is – at least, in our opinion – easily digested and a little less dry to read than most other business books out there. We've also written it in such a way that each of its five sections can stand on their own – that is, you don't have to read this book in order, or even in its entirety, to get what you need out of it. This means if you already have a blindingly brilliant CV, you can skip straight past Section 1 and go right on to Section 2.

WHO ARE WE?

What? Two words each weren't enough for you?

If you are curious about who we are and why we feel we can speak about the job search so authoritatively,* then let us introduce ourselves.

Having worked in recruitment for the past decade, Matt has helped literally thousands of people find a job and, during that time, has built up a reputation for filling hard-to-place roles, particularly in the sales in-dustry. Some of the candidates Matt has placed have ended up working for the likes of Google, Amazon,

*Prophetically, even, if the title is to be believed.

Goldman Sachs, Virgin and KPMG, to name just a few.

Since graduating from Queen Mary University of London in 2019 with a first-class degree in Drama, Huw has experienced his fair share of the *other* side of the job search. He has written a number of plays, short stories and is, as of this edition, now working on his first novel.

When Matt hired Huw at the start of 2020, it wasn't long before we decided to combine our strengths to create this book. To put it simply, Matt's the brains and Huw's the ... well, the more artistic brains.

BEFORE WE BEGIN

We'll get stuck into Section 1 soon. Before we do, however, we want to put a couple of things on the record.

Firstly, we want to state that everything you'll find in this book is simply technique. While, yes, we'll give you the occasional tip and/or trick that most job-seekers miss, you shouldn't think that within these pages you're going to discover the gigantic, shrouded secret that will land you your dream job with a single well-placed email. Said secret doesn't actually exist, as much as we'd like it to. The advice we're about to give you isn't magic, it's just best practice. But, just as a billion drops of water together make an ocean, when implemented, all these pieces of advice will give you a better chance than the vast majority of other applicants in your field.

Secondly, we want to talk about the importance of mindset. *Oh no,* we hear you say, *I've gone and picked up one of those self-help books by accident. I bet they'll tell me next that I have a worse chance of getting hired because I'm a Gemini.* Don't worry. We're not about to tell you that all you have to do is *believe in yourself* to be handed the perfect job. Unfortunately, that's not how the world works. However, we'd be remiss if we didn't give credit to the effect your mindset has on your chances. If two people with identical credentials walk into an interview, one of them an optimist and the other a defeatist, the job will undoubtedly go to the former. Now, there is a chance that the defeatist feels that way because this is the eighth interview they've been on this month. We understand that maintaining your resolve in the face of repetitive rejection can be incredibly draining (hell, both of us have experience of trying to break into the acting industry). We would stress, however, that you should try to let every application exist in a vacuum, unaffected by what has come before it or what might come after.

That said, we are aware that the words 'cheer up' never succeeded in actually improving anyone's mood. When you're applying to a multitude of jobs, fully aware of the often colossal competition, it can be almost impossible to believe that you have a chance. You begin asking yourself, *Why would they hire me? What makes me unique?* The best way to stop asking this question is, unsurprisingly, to answer it. If you take an afternoon to write down everything that you're good at, and all the unique experiences you have that others don't, you'll find it far easier to continue in the face of that competition. Doing this will also allow you to know which jobs you'd be better suited for, saving you the time you might waste applying for jobs that you wouldn't like or wouldn't be good at.

Finally, if you do sit down to figure out what you have to offer and end up finding the list worryingly short, we'd suggest changing that. Enrol in some on-line courses, watch some YouTube videos, read some books (after you finish this one, of course) and sharpen your skill set. If you can walk into an interview and confidently tell your interviewer about how you taught yourself to code in Python or received a certificate in graphic design online, the self-motivation and initiative it would have taken to achieve those things may end up doing more for you than any newly-acquired skills! What we're trying to say is that you'll struggle to convince an interviewer that you're worth hiring if you can't convince yourself of it first.

With all that out of the way, let's get started!

SECTION ONE

BUILDING YOUR
BULLETPROOF
CV

CHAPTER 1

WHY, THOUGH?

You might be wondering how we can fill 51 pages with CV advice. Perhaps this is because you're hoping we'll say something like, *When it comes down to it, all that really matters is you, so don't worry about formatting, length, or any of that pesky nonsense. Write from the heart.* Unfortunately, CVs are one of the few things in life that are better written from the brain.

As you're reading this book, you'll notice that we often can't resist the opportunity to tumble into an extended analogy. Some work quite well, while others might be a *tad* heavy-handed. The first of these analogies follows on the next page, and you can judge its quality for yourself:

Imagine you've decided to go shopping. You are looking to buy a jumper. Now, you have an idea of what you'd like in terms of colour, shape, material etc., but you're aware that perfection is an illusion so you're flexible on the details.

You walk along the high street looking at the shops, searching for ones that you think would be likely to sell the jumper you want. So, you walk past electronics shops, toy shops, restaurants and all the places that clearly do not sell jumpers.

You also walk past the places that might sell jumpers, but *definitely* not the kind you want. These shops are run-down with broken windows, misspelled signs and a musty smell that suggests they haven't been tidied since the late nineties. You kind of jog past these, slightly afraid.

There are clothes shops you stop and look at, considering that they *might* sell jumpers. You can't really tell, though, as there isn't anything in the shop window, and when you walk in, the place is so gigantic that you know that even if they *do* sell jumpers, it might take several months to locate them. You turn around and walk out.

That's when you see it – a shop whose sign says **JUMPERS JUMPERS JUMPERS** in giant, shiny letters. In the shop window, you see, believe it or not, jumpers! They're not just hanging there, either; they're modelled by mannequins of all shapes and sizes, *proving* that these jumpers are suitable for wear.

Even though you might not see the exact jumper you want in the window, you practically sprint into the shop, because you know that if that jumper is anywhere, it's going to be here. And if not, they're going to have the next best thing.

Now, what we've probably made painfully obvious is that in this scenario, you are a hiring manager or recruiter, the shops are CVs, and the ideal jumper is the ideal set of skills and experience that said hiring manager or recruiter will be looking for in a candidate.

See, those other shops may have actually had that perfect jumper, but no one is going to bother walking into every single shop on the high street on the off-chance they happen to stock what they want. No, they'll just go into the shops that already suggest that they do.

This is where your CV comes in.

You need to *suggest* that you have what your ideal employer is looking for. This comes across not only in what skills and experience you have, but in how you present that information; you don't want someone seeing that you sell jumpers, but end up turning away because they'll have to wade through a bunch of other things to find them.

The unfortunate truth is that, on average, recruiters will spend *six seconds* looking at a CV. That's how long you have to convince them to keep reading. *But how am I supposed to know what they're looking for?* Don't worry; that comes later. For now, we need to establish the basic *Dos* and *Don'ts* of Building Your Bulletproof CV.

CHAPTER 2

WHAT AND WHAT NOT TO DO

Before we go into detail with anything, we're going to start nice and simple with a bulleted list that clears up what you should and should not do whilst crafting that CV of yours.

DO

✓ Keep it concise. No more than two sides
✓ Omit unnecessary/protected information such as gender, age, ethnicity, religion etc.
✓ Begin sentences with verbs, rather than having everything in the first person ('Managed a team' instead of 'I was in charge of a team')

✓ Outline your career history with the most recent experience listed first, making sure to explain any gaps

✓ Bullet-point your achievements and responsibilities, giving more detail to more recent experience

✓ List your education and qualifications, again with the most recent listed first

✓ Include IT skills, spoken languages and relevant training

✓ Mention hobbies and interests, but keep them brief

✓ State that *Referees are available upon request*

✓ Check for errors yourself, as well as asking someone else to check for you

DON'T

✗ Ramble on for 18 pages (front and back) – your CV should consist of your selling points and nothing else

✗ Include a photo of yourself (unless necessary) – the interview goes to the best-looking CV, not the best-looking person

✗ Use clichés – avoid them like the plague. Don't bother telling them that you're a team player with excellent communication skills. Instead, let them infer it from your achievements and experience

✗ Embellish the truth or, worse, flat-out lie. Things

can easily be checked with referees and records, and one seemingly innocent untruth may unravel your whole application

✖ List every single process, package or project you've ever worked on, trained on, heard of, seen on a job specification or vaguely thought about

✖ Use graphics, tables or – God forbid – clipart. They look untidy at best and unsightly at worst, and even that's assuming the formatting holds together. Just don't

✖ Use lots of colours to make it look nice – more often than not, it's just jarring and confusing. If you must, use one other colour on the headings, but nothing too bright or pale, and always use black for body text

✖ Include inappropriate social media handles, especially if the content within may be held against you

✖ Use a strange font to try to stand out – if it takes any more effort than normal to read, recruiters won't bother to read it

✖ Shrink the font down to a subatomic size or widen the margins almost past the edge of the page in an effort to fit as much information in as possible

✖ Tack on pages from obscure testimonials, articles, newspaper clippings or brochures

✖ Submit your CV using the email you created at age 12 (so no xxn00b.sl4yer.42069xx@hotmail.co.uk addresses please)

Now, this doesn't quite cover everything because, if it did, this section would be two pages long. What it does do, however, is give you a pretty good check-list to run through when you come to build your CV so that you can ensure you're doing everything you should be and avoiding all those pitfalls that may hurt your chances.

CHAPTER 3

PREPARATION

All too often someone will sit down to write a CV by just popping their name at the top and bullet-pointing anything that comes to mind. The problem with not planning *how* you're going to write your CV is exactly the same as the one encountered having failed to plan a fictional story before you write it – you're going to end up with a piece of writing that repeats itself, misses out details and is rampant with inconsistencies. For this reason, planning and preparation are key.

The best way to write a CV is to write the story of your working life and then edit it down into a kind of CliffsNotes version – a synopsis or summary that gives recruiters and hiring managers all the important details without any unnecessary or irrelevant waffle.

Think of it this way: imagine you had to catch a friend up on your favourite TV show in its sixth season. If season four was all a dream sequence with no bearing on the plot, you would mention it in passing, but largely gloss over it. Similarly, you may have spent time in an industry that is no longer relevant to the role for which you're applying. By all means mention it in your CV to explain the gap, but don't spend too much time on it, since it doesn't affect your 'plot'.

Okay. With another analogy out of the way, let's move on.

TEMPLATING

First, a note about templating. Don't worry, we're not about to tell you that templating is lazy and evil and that you should never do it. Templating is actually a pretty good place to start. In fact, at the end of this section, you'll find a couple of templates we've put together in case you're struggling with formatting.

However, you need to remember that if you hope to stand out to a recruiter or hiring manager, your CV also has to. This means that it needs to be unique. So, yes, go ahead and use a template as a jumping-off point. Down the line, though, do make efforts to try to make it your own.

WORKING HISTORY

The first thing you need to do is write down your entire working history. This includes paid work, unpaid work, internships, volunteering, contract work – all of it. Write down your responsibilities and key achievements for each role. Remember, though, that your CV is not an autobiography, so this is not actually going directly into your CV. Create a separate file and write it there. This file is for you and you alone; it's your reference material from which you will pull any details you judge necessary or beneficial to include in your actual CV.

Why write it down, rather than just pulling pieces of it from your memory? Simply because the act of writing it down will help you to fill in any gaps or details you may not have realised were missing.

As this is just for you, you can format it however you'd like, but we'd recommend keeping it to a timeline style, rather than a huge chunk of prose. This way, when you come back to look for details, they'll be much easier to find.

REVERSE ENGINEERING

This step works best if you have a very specific job in mind for which you're applying. See, what a lot of people will do is write their CV and then go looking for job posts. Makes sense, right?

In fact, if you look for that job post *first* and then write your CV *afterwards*, this will allow you to do some crafty reverse engineering. What does this mean? Essentially, instead of hoping your CV fits that ideal job description, you can cleverly write it so that it already does.

At first glance, this may seem to some a little bit deceptive or manipulative. In reality, it's no different than a brand marketing the same product in different ways so that it appeals to specific demographics, rather than trying a single marketing campaign that attempts to cover as wide an audience as possible. In the same way that Nike will have a few different ads aimed at kids, teens and adults, you might have a few different CVs aimed at different roles. It's not about lying or embellishing (and again, *do not lie on your CV*), it's about emphasising different parts of the truth (skills, attributes, achievements, experience), depending on your audience.

For example, let's say that the only work experience you have is as a barista – which, given this book is aimed at those just beginning their career, may well be the case – and you've decided you want to get what we in this late-stage-capitalist productivity-centred society call a 'proper job'. As to the specifics of this job, you don't really care; all you want is that sweet

9-6 fluorescent-lit office life.

You apply to two industries: marketing and accounting.

In your marketing CV, you emphasise your skills on the chalkboard – your beautiful hand-drawn typography and renderings of pop-culture icons often sell coffees all by themselves. You also reference your ability to follow the trends in the café, knowing when to stock more of certain products depending on how popular you know they'll be over the next week/month. You big-up your interpersonal skills, remembering all the regulars' names, supervising the new staff, getting discounts from distributors (notice that you're backing up every claim with evidence – good work). You talk about all of this because you know that's the stuff a Head of Marketing will be on the lookout for.

Then you write your accounting CV. All that marketing stuff? Out the window. Now you talk about *numbers.* You would count up all the receipts at the end of the day, laughing in the face of those who suggested you use a calculator. During Covid-19 social distancing measures, you were easily able to keep track of the number of customers in the café at any given time. You could even remember the phone numbers of all your colleagues off by heart in case you needed to call someone in for cover.

You get the picture.

The point is that whilst all the information in both

the marketing and accounting CVs may have been true, neither was relevant to the other. If you placed all the information into one CV, a hiring manager for either industry would have to wade through lots of unnecessary detail to get through to the stuff that mattered to them.

Incidentally, this is why it's critical to know what you want to do. Now, this might be a scary question to some, but this doesn't have to mean 'What do you want to do *for the rest of your life?*' It doesn't even have to mean 'What do you want to do for the next five years?' It could be as simple as 'What could you see yourself as happy doing in a year's time?'

There doesn't have to be one answer to this question. In fact, if you believe there is only one answer to this question, you might have to do some re-evaluating. As long as you have a vague idea of what you're good at, what you enjoy, and what job can utilise these skills, you can begin to implement this technique.

Finally, to quote many a disgruntled spouse, *it's not just about what you say, it's how you say it.* By this, we don't mean that you should do what many do and labour over phrasing 'Screwed in a light bulb' as 'Supervised a project involving the rotary installation of specialised electronic equipment, resulting in the illumination of the office environment, considerably improving working conditions'. While there is certainly room for charging your sentences with a little more electricity – something we will cover later – what we're referring to here is the use of a lot of specific terms in a company's job description to outline what they want. What you can do as you're building your CV is lift some of these terms and place them directly into the CV.

For example, a company might say they're looking for someone who's 'team-oriented'. In your CV, you might have said you're 'a people person'. Those two terms basically mean the same thing, right? So why not use the one they've specified?

You can do this not just with traits, but with skills and even achievements (though it might be hard to make a Drama degree sound like a PhD in Chemical Engineering – no disrespect to Drama, of course; after all, that's what Huw did). We'll emphasise once more that *you must not lie or embellish*, but something that Huw learned during his Drama degree was that the beauty of language is that you can say the same thing in many different ways. Use this to your advantage.

CHAPTER 4

WHAT DO I WRITE IN MY CV?

And there it is: the most common question asked around the topic of CVs. It's understandable, of course, seeing as you never cover this topic in school aside from maybe a cursory glance. Everyone has a general idea that CVs should list education and experience, but after that people begin to get a little hazy. Should you include your hobbies? Referees? How far back do you need to go? Should you include that paper round? The primary school you went to?

This haziness comes down to the fact that there are no set rules regarding CVs – you can slap anything you want on that piece of paper and call it your curriculum vitae; no one is going to come and arrest you. Hell, if you wanted to, you could send that hiring manager the

BUILDING YOUR BULLETPROOF CV

entire screenplay for Star Wars Episode III – Revenge of the Sith and receive no ill consequences other than perhaps a somewhat confused response containing a distinct lack of a job offer.

Of course, as with any sandbox, this presents you with a lot of freedom, but little guidance. You can, however, use this to your advantage; whilst others are justifying the 'D' they got in GCSE Geography, you can focus purely on the things that are going to help you get that job, ignoring anything that is irrelevant or un-helpful. We've told you not to lie or embellish, but as long as you don't leave any glaring gaps that will come up in interview, you can *omit* anything you want. So, if you don't think that your AS level in Dance is going to help you get that job in data analytics, go ahead and leave it out (again, no disrespect to Dance; we both wish we could manage more than an awkward robot).

So, in terms of details, it's completely up to you. When it comes to structure, let us help you out. What we'll state now is that you do not have to put these sections in the order in which we present them. If you're a recent graduate with no professional expe-rience, we'd suggest putting your education before whatever retail or hospitality experience you have. If you've got a year or so in a professional environment under your belt, then put that first. It's all about what is going to put you in the best light.

EDUCATION

The general rule we give for Education/Academics is to give your last two qualifications: if you were educated in the UK, that could be GCSEs* and A levels, A levels and undergrad, undergrad and master's, etc. Of course, as with any rule, there are exceptions. Namely, in this case, if you've completed a course in the past that, if left out, would create a questionable gap in your CV. Remember, gaps in your CV will always be noticed and will always come up in interview.

WORKING HISTORY

When it comes to how far back to go with your work history, again it's about gaps. If you did retail and bar work while you were at university, you could decide to leave this out without it creating any gaps. However, if you left uni and *then* did those jobs, their omission would raise questions. Similarly, if you had a side gig along with your 9-5, you don't necessarily have to declare that. But, if you took a few months off from that 9-5 to pursue that side gig, those months would need

*If you are including your GCSEs, you don't need to list every subject, just list your grades (e.g. 2 A*s, 3 As, 3 Bs, 1 C) and then mention what you got for Maths, English and anything directly relevant to the role.

to be explained.

Put simply, as soon as you leave education, each period of time needs to be explained, with perhaps a couple of months' wiggle room for finding a job.

But I spent three months sweating around South East Asia in an attempt to find myself!

That's great! But make sure you mention it.

As for what to write for each job, there's a simple formula to help you stand out as organised and detailed without being too waffly:

1. Company Title
2. Dates (month and year – don't worry about the day)
3. Short Company Description (A recruiter will google the companies you worked for, so save them the effort and do it for them.)
4. Job Title (This doesn't have to be your official title – if you can write something that is close to the job you're applying for while still being accurate, go for it.)
5. Three Responsibilities, beginning with verbs ('Making coffee' rather than 'I was responsible for making coffee')
6. Two 'Proven' Skills (Give a skill you used in the role and an example of how and when you used it.)
7. One Key Achievement (We'll talk more about these soon, but this will be the most important and relevant thing you achieved at that company. Relevant

is the operative word – if you saved a person's life at work but are applying for a financial role, they might rather hear about the time you cut 20% from the electricity bill by replacing all the light bulbs with 'rustic' gas lamps.)

Across all of these use facts and figures whenever you can and name-drop any recognisable brands you've worked with, as they will add validity to your statements.

A note about your responsibilities – you should only state responsibilities that are relevant and aren't already obvious; if you've done bar work, we already *know* that you served drinks, liaised with customers, cleaned up, handled money, etc. If, however, on top of that you sometimes managed the busy pub all by yourself, that would be worth mentioning. Do this for whichever jobs you deem relevant or important, but don't worry about doing it for every single one if you don't have the space for it.

KEY ACHIEVEMENTS & CORE SKILLS

Ask any CV coach and they will tell you that the most important thing about a CV is your skills. They're not wrong, but simply chucking them into a bullet-pointed list is not only boring, it's dubious. When you say you're an IT wizard, how are we supposed to know if that means you eat Raspberry Pi for breakfast*, or just that you can Google your way through an Excel doc?

That's where key achievements come in. This is your way to provide *evidence* for your claims.

Here's how it works: Take a look at the document where you've written your full working history. From that, write down a list of anything that could be classified as an achievement:

- What qualifications/awards have you attained?
- What important projects have you completed using your skills?
- What problems have you solved or avoided entirely?
- What challenges have you overcome?
- What experience/knowledge have you accumulated?

The next step is to look at the job description given by that ideal company and do some of the reverse engineering we talked about earlier. What skills and traits are they looking for? Write these down in a list, too.

For each skill or trait that the company lists, search through your key achievements to find something that demonstrates it. If you can't find anything, have a think about what you could put in its place – this is good

*If you don't get that joke, look it up, because it's *excellent*.

preparation for interviews, where you will be asked to show you have these skills. Remember only to put in the achievements that are relevant to the role, rather than risk coming across as if you're bragging.

Then, put down a couple of core skills. These should be skills that your key achievements prove, and should match the main skills specified in the job description. As for your other skills that may be relevant but less pertinent, such as languages or IT skills, they will come later.

This section should come right at the top, just after your personal statement.

PERSONAL STATEMENT

Ah yes, the dreaded personal statement, the point at which we all realise just how boring and unemployable we are. We've all been there, staring at a blinking cursor wondering why it's so difficult to sum up our entire personality in a couple of sentences.

Here's the thing about the recruiter or hiring manager that has just opened your CV: they don't care about your personality. Not yet, anyway. At the point where they reach your personal statement, all you are to them is a name at the top of a piece of paper. If they go on to read that you are a *fun, friendly person who works hard and is always on time*, they are still not going to care.

Remember the fact from earlier: you have six seconds on average to prove to the person reading your CV that it is worth their time to keep reading. So how do you do that? Easy: show them you have what they want.

First comes your career objective. You need to state early in the sentence that the job they are recruiting for is the job that you want; this way, they know that you're forward-thinking and passionate, and that you haven't just blindly cast your net in hopes of a response.

Even better, put your career objective as a job that you could *progress* to from that position. For example, you might be applying for a role as a Sales Executive, but write in your personal statement that you're an 'Aspiring Sales Manager'. One piece of advice here, however, is not to go further than one step below whomever is doing the hiring;* you don't want it to look like you're out to steal their job!

Better still would be to have a look at the job description to see if they mention anything about career progression, and use this in your application.

Next, summarise your best and most relevant key achievements, whether that's your degree, some other

---

*You should always know who's going to be reading your CV. It only takes a quick look on LinkedIn to find a company's staff page, and from there the HR department.

qualification, your professional experience – anything that demonstrates you have what's required. Integrate this with something about your core skills to paint a picture of your suitability for the role.

Finally, state your motivations. That could be building your experience, seeking a change of pace, making a career shift – you need to let them know *why* you're applying for this job (unfortunately, 'I need cash' won't look great, however true it is).

This is an introduction, so don't waste time elaborating on things you're going to repeat later. Keep it two to three sentences long. If you're still unsure of what to put in it, there are some templates at the end of this section that might help you out.

ADDITIONAL INFORMATION

This will go after your work history and education, and is where you'll put all those other skills that you left out earlier:

✓ Completed training courses (including online, such as Skillshare/Udemy)

✓ Languages (write as 'Spanish (intermediate)', 'German (fluent)', 'French (basic)', 'English (native)', etc.) Please don't just write that you're fluent in English if it's the only language you speak.

✓ IT Skills. Most will assume you're competent with Microsoft Word and PowerPoint, but if you're skilled at Excel it's worth mentioning alongside other pro-grammes that may be relevant to the role such as Adobe software, CRMs, etc. Add the software and your competency, similar to the languages.

HOBBIES AND INTERESTS

You have to be a little careful here. See, there are many of us for whom when someone asks us our hobbies, we open the door to that part of our brain to find it pretty bare. Instead, we borrow things from the adjacent 'What I Do in My Spare Time' room and hope no one will notice the difference. So, we say our hobbies include *cinema, literature* and *photography* when really it's just *browsing Netflix, scrolling through Reddit* and *posting selfies on Instagram*, all wearing fancy hats.

The problem with this is that recruiters and hiring managers can spot these hats from a mile away. So, if you only list these, not only have you presented yourself as boring and lazy, you've also failed to deceive them.

Okay, that might sound a little harsh. You have to understand, however, that everything on your CV *has* to aid you in getting that job. Telling people your favourite sitcom is *Community* does nothing but show that you have good taste which, while nice, does not make you more employable.

Hobbies and interests are your opportunity to show that even in your off-time, you are the ideal candidate for the job. Let's say you're applying for a job as a graphic designer, and you happen to moderate a forum where people post their ideas for flags of countries in fantasy books. Or maybe you're looking to be a marketeer for an airline, and you run your own travel blog dedicated to the wallpapers of the hotel rooms you stay in. It's about coming off as interesting, active, and passionate.

That said, it doesn't necessarily have to be related to the job, as long as it fulfils the 'interesting' and 'active' aspects. Playing a sport, for example, shows that you're competitive and mindful about physical fitness, which many companies find desirable (bonus points if it's a team sport).

And, no, Fifa doesn't count.

As a final point, if you actually *are* interested in cinema/literature/photography to the point of it being a hobby, that is absolutely fine. Just make sure that you provide evidence, like stating your favourite film festival, your opinion for most underrated author, your favourite photographic trend, etc.

But I don't have any real hobbies, I don't play sports and I'm not really interested in anything worth writing about.

This is a very common predicament. Our response is to say with as much love as we can manage: Get a life.

Not to turn this book into a self-help motivational snooze-fest, but having *actual* hobbies and things that you just do for the joy of it is not just good for your CV. It's good for *you*. Whether it's creative or constructive, or just something to gather knowledge about, finding something that is *yours* that you can do simply to relax and have fun will help in many ways, such as reducing stress, and increasing fulfilment, and may be a way to find like-minded individuals. Using it to help get a job is just a nice bonus. Right, enough of that.

REFERENCES

This is going to be a short paragraph for a short section of your CV. Do not give your full references right away. By all means have them at the ready (and do ask a person's permission, they'll be less likely to give a good reference if they're surprised by the request), but all you need to put on your CV is 'References available upon request.' As for how many, three is a good number, but two will be fine if you can't manage a third.

PERSONAL INFORMATION

All you need here are your email address and phone number at the top of the page, with perhaps a *general* location (i.e. 'London', 'NYC', etc.). You can, if you'd like, include a link to your LinkedIn page as well (check out Section 2 for LinkedIn advice). You don't need your age, gender, ethnicity, disability information, or anything like that – although it is illegal to discriminate based on these characteristics, unfortunately it does still happen, more often in subtle ways,* so best not to give them the chance.

And that's it! Once you've got all of that information down, it's time to optimise your language so that it really jumps off the page.

*A BBC article from January 2019 reported that in the UK, applicants with names related to ethnic minority backgrounds had to send, on average, 60% more CVs before being called to interview, with those of Middle Eastern or north African heritage having to send upwards of 90% more applications than their White British counterparts with identical CVs.

CHAPTER 5

LANGUAGE OPTIMISATION

We mentioned earlier that it isn't just what you say, but how you say it that matters. This is true in a number of ways. Firstly, as we said before, there's using language that matches what the company uses in its job advert. This increases SEO (Search Engine Optimisation), making your CV easier to find for recruiters, as they will be searching specifically for the terms in that job advert. In addition to this, there are more ways you can improve your language to make your CV really *pop*. Like other advice within this book, these tips are not revolutionary. Instead, they are subtle edits that will simply tune your language so that it strikes a nicer chord.

PASSIVE VOICE

Use of the passive voice is a trap that many appli-cants will fall into when writing about their achievements and responsibilities. If you don't know what the passive voice is, then we'll demonstrate with two ways of saying the same thing:

1. My brother and I were involved in an altercation during which his leg was fractured.
2. I attacked my brother and shattered his femur.

Hopefully, the difference between these two statements is obvious. In case it isn't, we'll explain. In the first example, the action within the statement appears just to happen by itself while my brother and I are present. In the second, it is clear that I am the one who took action and broke my brother's leg. The language is also softened in the first example ('altercation' instead of 'attacked', 'fractured' instead of 'shattered').

You will see the passive voice used very often in news articles in an attempt to present an unbiased or uncharged account of an event, rather than place blame on any particular person or group. This is a problem, as it relieves that person or group of any accountability or responsibility, as well as downplaying the severity of events.

Okay, but why does this matter to my CV?

It matters because you *want* to give yourself

responsibility and accountability for your actions, rather than suggesting they just happened *to* you. You also want to make them sound exciting and important, not dull and blunted.

Many applicants get so caught up in writing their CVs in a "formal" way, that they deliberately downplay their language because they believe it looks more 'professional'. One example might be to say 'I was responsible for the sale of products, and for offering upgrades where possible' rather than 'I sold products according to customers' needs, and often persuaded them to purchase larger packages'. Both sentences say the same thing. The difference is whether the action was *caused* by you, or simply occurred *around* you. It's a subtle change, but it makes a *big* difference.

ACTION VERBS

What's the difference between 'assisted' and 'influenced'? 'Made' and 'created'? 'Spoke with' and 'entertained'? 'Wrote' and 'authored'?

We could go on. Whilst there might be small differences in the meanings of these words, the main gap is in how *interesting* they are. Just as with the example before, *regaling* an audience about how you *shattered* someone's leg is going to spark a lot more excitement than *talking* about *fracturing* it.

Once you have your CV written, be sure to go through and sprinkle in some relevant action verbs (but be careful not to go overboard).

There's a great guide to this on Glassdoor's website: www.glassdoor.com/blog/resume-action-verbs/

Another piece of advice is to start your sentences with the verb, rather than have everything start with 'I'. They know who you're writing about.

With your language all polished, it's time for finishing touches!

CHAPTER 6

WRAPPING IT UP

Now that all of the main text and formatting of your CV is complete, we'll just give you a few quick tips to tie it up with a nice little bow.

- Run your CV through *Grammarly* or a similar service to check the language. *Hemingway* is another useful tool.

- If required, don't include portfolios in the CV itself – it might be rejected by an ATS (Applicant Tracking System) if the file size is too large. Add links to them instead.

- You may also add links to any articles that relate to your achievements.

- Check that all links to portfolios/LinkedIn profiles/articles actually work.

- Save your CV under the file name '[First Name] | [Last Name] CV'. This way, when you attach it to emails, it's clear what it is and who it's from (and, no, saying 'curriculum vitae' instead of 'CV' won't make you look clever).
- Save it as a .doc or .docx file. If you save it as an image file such as a JPEG or PNG, it might get rejected by an ATS. PDFs will probably be fine if they don't have any strange formatting, but for safety it's best to go with your bog standard Word file.
- Before you save it, though, make sure to link your video CV.

Wait, my what?

CHAPTER 7

AN INTRODUCTION TO VIDEO CVS

So you want me to read this thing out on video now?

No, no one wants to watch that. A Video CV is not meant to replace your written CV, just to supplement it. They've become much more commonplace over the last few years as a way to add a bit more personality to the application process while giving an overview of your skills, experience and ambitions. They can either be uploaded to a hosting site and linked to, or alternatively sent directly to the company as a video file.

Before we get into the process of creating a Video CV, however, we'll run through some pro's and con's of having one, because while, for some, they might be the factor that wins over a hiring manager, for others, it could cause their application to get tossed in the bin.

PROS

✓ Stand Out – While rising in popularity, video CVs are still by no means common. Using one at all will differentiate you from most.

✓ Be Unique – Video CVs are a great opportunity to be creative, much more so than a standard paper CV. Fun editing techniques, sound design, graphics, cinematography... you could really go wild if you'd like. Especially good for artistic roles.

✓ Be You – It's difficult (though not impossible) to convey your personality on a paper CV. On video, it's much easier.

✓ Showcase Skills – If you're applying for a job in which communication skills, public speaking, confidence, or even video editing skills will be appreciated, this is your chance to prove that you've got that stuff in spades.

✓ Give Evidence – It doesn't have to be just your face the entire time. As you talk, you could show B-roll images or video from your achievements/portfolio, proving the claims you make about yourself and your work.

✓ Display Enthusiasm – It takes far more effort to record a personal video CV than it does simply to hit a 'One Click Apply' button. With this, you can demonstrate how eager you are to apply.

CONS

✖ Bias – Unfortunately, some of those protected characteristics we talked about earlier (e.g. race, gender, age, ability) become obvious on video, potentially opening you up to unfair treatment.

✖ Not for Everyone – A video CV might make you stand out for the wrong reasons; if you're awkward on camera, uncomfortable presenting, or if your communication skills are lacking, then it may work against you.

✖ Short Form – Video CVs are (ideally) quite short, which may mean you don't have time to talk about all the things that make you an ideal candidate.

✖ Time-Consuming – With the setting-up, the scripting, the filming itself and the editing, video CVs take a while to create. Some recruiters believe this time would be better spent perfecting your paper CV.

✖ Potential Perturbation – Some employers might find a video CV irritating (remember, some of them will spend barely 10 seconds looking at your paper CV, let alone watch a video for 2 minutes). It's a case-by-case basis that depends on the industry, the company and possibly even the hiring manager themselves. Use your own judgement to decide what you think would be appreciated.

Ultimately, this will be different for everyone, but our experience tells us, on the whole, video CVs are a great way to stand out and demonstrate your worth.

CHAPTER 8

SETTING UP YOUR VIDEO CV

If you've decided that the pros of a video CV out-weigh the cons (which, in most cases, we believe they do), then it'd be worth knowing how to prepare your personal film set to get the best results.

CAMERA

You don't need to go out and buy an expensive DSLR, or anything like that – most smartphone cameras will do a perfectly good job. Film in landscape, not portrait, as this most likely will not be viewed on a phone. In the event that it is, a phone is easier to turn sideways than a computer monitor.

BACKGROUND

You don't want anything too distracting going on behind you, so we'd recommend avoiding rooms where people will be walking through the background. It's also wise not to film in front of posters of movies/TV shows/celebrities as it can come across as unprofessional. A plain wall, a bookcase or some tasteful art is ideal, especially if it's something relevant to the role.

LIGHTING

Exactly how much effort you want to put into this is up to you, but a good rule of thumb is to avoid direct sunlight as it's quite harsh. Instead, draw the curtain or blind and then turn on a lamp aimed towards (but not directly at) your face. Don't worry too much about this, though; you just need your face to be clearly and consistently visible and the room not to be plunged into darkness.

ANGLE

We've all accidentally opened up our front camera to be treated to a less than flattering worm's-eye view of our unsmiling mug. From this experience alone, we know that the angle at which you take photos – and, by extension, videos – matters. Get your camera as close to eye level as you can. If that means having to sit down, that's absolutely fine.

DISTRACTIONS

If you live with any other people, make sure they're aware of what you're doing – you don't want to be in the middle of a take when Mum asks you to bring down your dirty pants to be washed.

Similarly, as much as we all love pets, shut yours out of the room if there's a chance they'll wander into shot.

It's also worth switching your phone onto do not disturb mode, especially if you're using it to film. You don't want a stray notification to ruin a take.

SOUND

Get as close to silence as possible. Try to film away from road-adjacent rooms if car noise is going to be an issue, and ensure there's no music or TV playing in the house loud enough to come through on video.

To improve sound quality, try placing soft materials (cushions, blankets etc.) behind the camera to reduce the reverb in the room and make it sound clearer.

DRESS CODE

This depends on the kind of companies you're applying for. You might need to dress right up to the nines, or you might be fine with a simple smart blouse or button-up shirt. A good way of telling what you should wear is to look at the companies' 'Team' or 'About Us' pages and see what people are wearing in their staff photos. While there's a chance that they dressed smarter than usual for picture day, it's very unlikely that they dressed down. Whatever you do, don't wear hoodies, graphic T-shirts, pyjamas or, for whatever reason, nothing at all.

CHAPTER 9

WHAT TO SAY IN YOUR VIDEO CV

Video CVs are tricky things to make. You want to come across professionally, but inject enough personality so as not to appear robotic. You want to say enough so you can sell yourself, but not so much that you end up boring the viewer and wasting everyone's time. We recommend that your Video CV be between 45 seconds and two minutes, preferably leaning towards one minute.

In terms of what you need to say, you don't have to try to regurgitate all the details you've already listed in your paper CV. This video is more of an overview, an introduction that will help build familiarity. If a hiring manager can already feel familiar with you when they bring you in for interview, you've made a step towards being trusted by them. If they feel they can trust you, they're more likely to hire you.

So, as an overview or introduction, you should mention:

- Your name
- Your career objective
- Your most relevant experience
- One key achievement
- The core skills used to achieve it

THE CHEEKY CHEAT SCRIPT

If you're still scratching your head over what exactly to say, don't worry. We've got you covered.

What follows is a pretty standard script that you can steal, fill in the blanks and film. You don't have to follow it word for word (in fact, depending on how popular this book gets, it may be wise not to), but it's a good scaffold on which to base your video CV.

Hi, I'm [Name].

My career objective is to excel in a [Ideal Company Culture] environment that will allow me to utilise my experience in [Skill 1] and [Skill 2].

Ideally, my perfect role would be a [Ideal Future Promotion] in a [Ideal Company Persona] within the next [Realistic but Ambitious Timeframe].

During my time at [Most Relevant/Recent Experience], I

was able to supersede expectations. My key achievement was [Key Achievement], which was attributed to my skills in [Skill 3] and [Skill 4].

I would love to meet you to tell you more about why I'd be perfect for this role.

I can't wait to meet you.

Once the script is filmed, pop the footage into Movie Maker or iMovie, depending on whether you're a PC or Mac user. You don't have to be an Oscar-worthy editor; all you need to do is snip out any ums and ahs or awkward pauses so that you come across as best as possible.

In addition to this, you can include any examples of your work if you're an artist, or any images of you 'in action' in your past role if relevant. It's a visual medium, so take advantage of that!

Once edited, export it as an .mp4 file, as it's the easiest video file to open. Like your paper CV, save it as '[First Name] | [Last Name] Video CV'.

With that done, congratulations! You've completed both your paper CV and your video CV and are ready to send them off.

CHAPTER 10

CONCLUSION

We hope you've learned a thing or two about how to craft your Bulletproof CV. One last thing we'd recommend is to flick back to Chapter 2 and run through that *Dos* and *Don't*s list one more time as a final flight check.

After that, well done! You've perfected what is arguably your most important job-seeking asset. We'll leave you with a couple of templates you might want to use, depending on whether or not you already have some professional experience. We'll also pop in a couple of templates of personal statements for varying stages in your professional life. We'll see you in Section 2: **Becoming a LinkedIn All-Star!**

email@address.com   LinkedIn Link   Phone Number

First Name Surname

Career objective, summary of your key achievements and core skills, to sell yourself right away. Briefly mention the types of roles you've previously worked in and how these will help you to excel in this role.

Achievements & Core Skills

- Relevant achievement 1
- Relevant achievement 2
- Core Skill 1

- Relevant Achievement 3
- Relevant achievement 4
- Core skill 2

Work History

COMPANY NAME – *Date-Date*
Overview on the company, what they do and with whom they are associated. Use the names of brands, clients and partners if applicable. Any stats and figures you can give will be helpful, too.

Job Title
- Responsibility 1 – list a responsibility that you had in the business. Mention brand names/partners/numbers if able. Add helpful descriptive details.
- Responsibility 2 – list a responsibility that you had in the business. Mention brand names/partners/numbers if able. Add helpful descriptive details.
- Responsibility 3 – list a responsibility that you had in the business. Mention brand names/partners/numbers if able. Add helpful descriptive details.
- Skill 1 proved – list a relevant skill, where you were able to use it and a successful outcome of using it. Names/partners/number & details.
- Skill 2 proved – list a relevant skill, where you were able to use it and a successful outcome of using it. Names/partners/number & details.
- Key Achievement

COMPANY NAME – *Date-Date*
Overview on the company, what they do and with whom they are associated. Use the names of brands, clients and partners if applicable. Any stats and figures you can give will be helpful, too.

Job Title
- Responsibility 1 – list a responsibility that you had in the business. Mention brand names/partners/numbers if able. Add helpful descriptive details.
- Responsibility 2 – list a responsibility that you had in the business. Mention brand names/partners/numbers if able. Add helpful descriptive details.
- Responsibility 3 – list a responsibility that you had in the business. Mention brand names/partners/numbers if able. Add helpful descriptive details.
- Skill 1 proved – list a relevant skill, where you were able to use it and a successful outcome of using it. Names/partners/number & details.
- Skill 2 proved – list a relevant skill, where you were able to use it and a successful outcome of using it. Names/partners/number & details.
- Key Achievement

EXPERIENCED CV TEMPLATE – PAGE 1

email@address.com   LinkedIn Link   Phone Number

First Name Surname

COMPANY NAME – *Date-Date*
Overview on the company, what they do and with whom they are associated. Use the names of brands, clients and partners if applicable. Any stats and figures you can give will be helpful, too.

Job Title
- Responsibility 1 – list a responsibility that you had in the business. Mention brand names/partners/numbers if able. Add helpful descriptive details.
- Responsibility 2 – list a responsibility that you had in the business. Mention brand names/partners/numbers if able. Add helpful descriptive details.
- Responsibility 3 – list a responsibility that you had in the business. Mention brand names/partners/numbers if able. Add helpful descriptive details.
- Skill 1 proved – list a relevant skill, where you were able to use it and a successful outcome of using it. Names/partners/number & details.
- Skill 2 proved – list a relevant skill, where you were able to use it and a successful outcome of using it. Names/partners/number & details.
- Key Achievement

Relevant Information and Skills
Language 1 (level), language 2 (level)
IT Skills: relevant software, specialist software

Education
Name of institution of highest qualification
Grade, Subject
Relevant info, e.g. thesis title, relevant modules

Name of institution of second highest qualification
Grade, Subject
Relevant info, e.g. thesis title, relevant modules

Voluntary Work
Organisation name – role, description of role, relevance to role applied for

Hobbies and Interests
Hobby 1 – a small line about your hobby and why it's important to you, to build familiarity

Hobby 2 – a small line about your hobby and why it's important to you, to build familiarity

email@address.com　　　　　LinkedIn Link　　　　　Phone Number

First Name Surname

Career objective, summary of your key achievements and core skills, to sell yourself right away. Briefly mention the types of roles you've previously worked in and how these will help you to excel in this role.

Achievements & Core Skills

- Relevant achievement 1
- Relevant achievement 2
- Core Skill 1
- Relevant Achievement 3
- Relevant achievement 4
- Core skill 2

Education

Name of institution of highest qualification – *Date-Date*
Grade, Subject
Relevant info, e.g. thesis title, relevant modules

Name of institution of second highest qualification – *Date-Date*
Grade, Subject
Relevant info, e.g. thesis title, relevant modules

Achievements & Extra Curricular Activities
- List any societies or outstanding work, emphasising any committee roles

Work History

COMPANY NAME – *Date-Date*
Overview on the company, what they do and with whom they are associated. Use the names of brands, clients and partners if applicable. Any stats and figures you can give will be helpful, too.

Job Title
- Responsibility 1 – list a responsibility that you had in the business. Mention brand names/ partners/numbers if able. Add helpful descriptive details.
- Responsibility 2 – list a responsibility that you had in the business. Mention brand names/ partners/numbers if able. Add helpful descriptive details.
- Responsibility 3 – list a responsibility that you had in the business. Mention brand names/ partners/numbers if able. Add helpful descriptive details.
- Skill 1 proved – list a relevant skill, where you were able to use it and a successful outcome of using it. Names/partners/number & details.
- Skill 2 proved – list a relevant skill, where you were able to use it and a successful outcome of using it. Names/partners/number & details.
- Key Achievement

email@address.com   LinkedIn Link   Phone Number

First Name Surname

COMPANY NAME – *Date-Date*
Overview on the company, what they do and with whom they are associated. Use the names of brands, clients and partners if applicable. Any stats and figures you can give will be helpful, too.

Job Title
- Responsibility 1 – list a responsibility that you had in the business. Mention brand names/partners/numbers if able. Add helpful descriptive details.
- Responsibility 2 – list a responsibility that you had in the business. Mention brand names/partners/numbers if able. Add helpful descriptive details.
- Responsibility 3 – list a responsibility that you had in the business. Mention brand names/partners/numbers if able. Add helpful descriptive details.
- Skill 1 proved – list a relevant skill, where you were able to use it and a successful outcome of using it. Names/partners/number & details.
- Skill 2 proved – list a relevant skill, where you were able to use it and a successful outcome of using it. Names/partners/number & details.
- Key Achievement

Additional Work Experience
ROLE 1 – *Date-Date* – briefly summarise role, listing only what is relevant to the role for which you are applying

ROLE 2 – *Date-Date* – briefly summarise role, listing only what is relevant to the role for which you are applying

ROLE 3 – *Date-Date* – briefly summarise role, listing only what is relevant to the role for which you are applying

Relevant Information and Skills
Language 1 (level), language 2 (level)
IT Skills: relevant software, specialist software

Voluntary Work
Organisation name – role, description of role, relevance to role applied for

Hobbies and Interests
Hobby 1 – a small line about your hobby and why it's important to you, to build familiarity

Hobby 2 – a small line about your hobby and why it's important to you, to build familiarity

PERSONAL STATEMENT TEMPLATES

SCHOOL LEAVER

Future [Desired Role] who is highly motivated and hard working. Recently completed [GCSEs/A Levels], excelling in [Best Two Subjects]. Seeking [Role Level & Role Applied For] to strengthen upon core [Interest, e.g. Business, Communications] interest and start a career as a [Role].

GRADUATE

Upcoming [Desired Role] who excelled in [Previous Experience] and achieved [Main Achievement] down to excellent [Core Skill 1] and meticulous [Core Skill 2]. Proudly gained a [Degree Class] in [Degree Subject] from the prestigious [University]. Excited to use [Experience/Degree] to become a vital and valuable asset to your business.

UNEMPLOYED/REDUNDANCY

Successful [Desired Role] with over [X] years' experience in [Previous Role]. Proven track record of success, including [Key Achievements 1 + 2]. Looking to re-establish myself as a valuable asset in [Desired Role] and continue with my high-performance mentality.

CAREER BREAK

Future [Career Objective] who is highly motivated and experienced in [Previous Role]. Overachieved in last role with [Key Achievement 1] and wanting to transfer that knowledge to [Company] after a short gap to [Career Break Reason]. Looking for career-driven role to showcase my [Core Skills 1 + 2].

CAREER CHANGE

Excited to become [Career Objective]. With key achievements of [Key Achievements 1 + 2] as a [Previous Role] demonstrating excellence in [Core Skills 1 + 2]. Now looking to build on [Core Skills 3 + 4] and become [Desired Role]. With a wealth of transferable knowledge and a newfound passion for [New Industry], I will be an asset to your team.

SECTION TWO

BECOMING A LINKEDIN ALL-STAR

CHAPTER 1

THINKIN' LINKEDIN

Different social media sites have different jobs. Instagram is for trading envy over each other's clothes/meals/talents/holidays/bodies/partners; Facebook is for hearing about all your vague acquaintances' new babies, weddings and funerals; Twitter is for debating the intricacies of the failings of the American political system with someone who is just as clueless about it as you are; Tik-Tok is for lip-syncing to other people's comedy sketches and thinking it counts as being an influencer.

So what's LinkedIn's job? Put simply, LinkedIn is for proving to strangers that you're *definitely very success-ful.* Doing this well is doubly important when you're looking for a job, and doubly difficult if you're doing so from an unemployed starting position. You've some-how got to communicate that the fact you don't have a job right now is either deliberate, for purposes of personal and professional growth, or one of life's great mysteries.

At this point, you would be justified in wanting to hang the sense of it and avoid LinkedIn entirely, relying instead on your CV and sunny disposition to get you a job. Unfortunately, this is the 2020s, and LinkedIn has become indispensable as an online platform for professionals. The simple fact is that having a good LinkedIn profile is going to make your job search in-finitely easier than if you were to have no profile at all (or, even worse, a bad one).

LinkedIn was acquired by Microsoft in 2016 for $26.2 billion and as of 2021 has over 750 million users. It didn't earn all that money, however, just through ad-vertising revenue.

When it comes to LinkedIn and, by extension, social media as a whole, we like to think of ourselves as in control. It seems like we've been kindly gifted this free platform that we get to use to our hearts' content for no reason other than because we deserve something nice once in a while.

The problem is one that has become more and more common in recent years: if you are handed something for free that could easily have been sold to you, con-sider that you are not the customer, but the commodity.

It's no secret that Facebook sells your data – the 2018 Cambridge Analytica scandal was worldwide news. It raised questions about people's right to privacy and the dangers of social media's influence on the opinions of the population. It's important to know, however, that it isn't just Facebook. It's *everyone*. There was also the introduction of GDPR in 2018, which, among other things, meant that companies had to start informing people of how they would use their data (we're sure you remember all those emails). What this ended up boiling down to, though, was just another 'I agree' button to click blindly, following countless Terms and Conditions contracts before it. Just because companies started telling people all this stuff, it didn't mean those people started listening.

We like to think of the whole situation this way:

You get given a ticket to a brand-new island resort. It looks amazing and all your friends are going. The best part is that everything is totally free – accommodation, transport, food and drink, activities, amenities; you don't have to pay a single penny. Sure, there are some billboards dotted around, but no one is forcing you to look at them (although it is a bit weird that they seem always to be advertising something you were talking about only yesterday).

You find out one day, however, that the whole time you've been at this resort there have been hidden cameras everywhere – cameras in the streets, on the beach, in the restaurants, the pool, the hotel, your room. The company that owns the resort has been recording all your conversations with your friends, even the ones you thought were private. The drinks may be free, but they've been keeping track of what you order, how many and how often. They've also been monitoring your schedule, keeping notes of when you get up, how much time you spend at the beach, in the pool or on the golf course, and cross-referencing that against how much you told your friends you enjoyed yourself there. They've used this data to determine what kind of a person you are based on your age, gender, nationality, sexuality, political leanings, even your favourite TV shows.

They haven't just gathered this data for the fun of it, either. The resort has used it to softly wall you into an area of the island where you'll see only people the company reckons you'll get on with, keeping you away from those you might disagree with, in case you end up having a bad time and leaving the island. They've been selling your data to other companies, too. Turns out that's why all those billboards seemed eerily relevant: not everyone sees the same ones.

When you find this all out, you are outraged! You feel used and violated, like a character in some sick game of The Sims! You leave the island, vowing never to return. Many of your friends do the same.

A couple of weeks go by, and you receive an envelope. Inside is a letter from the resort apologising profusely for this abuse of power while simultaneously claiming that since what they did wasn't technically illegal, it was absolutely fine. Besides, it is illegal to do it without telling you now, so here they are, telling you, inviting you back to the island. They've sent a second envelope that's thicker than War and Peace, containing reams of paper explaining exactly what they do and how they do it. You can't be bothered to read all that paper, but you know all your friends are going back, so you just say 'screw it' and pack your bags without even opening the second envelope.

Back on the island, you don't necessarily see the cameras, but you can spot all the places they'd be. You start to wonder if you're paranoid for suspecting the birds of being spy drones. For a while, you and your friends are careful not to discuss anything on the island you wouldn't want heard by a third party. But this only lasts a short while before you give up the effort and resume walking around your hotel room in the nude.

Eventually, you even come to be grateful for the billboards: at least you're being shown stuff you might actually want.

And this is where we find ourselves: we all know the cameras are there, but we try our best to ignore them.

So why have we gone off on this tangent? Well, when it comes to other social media sites, your personal data influences only what you see in terms of news and adverts. On LinkedIn, however, it also determines who sees *you*.

See, LinkedIn has a number of different sides to it, only one of which is the social networking platform that most see. Its other sides include some products that it sells to different companies, most of which utilise its most valuable asset: you.

Here's a list of some of the products LinkedIn sells, with a little explanation of what they're for:

- Marketing Developer Platform – This is a platform that allows companies to do things like create targeted ad campaigns, automate certain processes and generate 'leads' (people who fit a defined profile that might be open to what they're selling).
- Sales Navigator – This is a tool that salespeople use to look for potential clients.
- Analytics – This is the name given to the statistics LinkedIn collects related to trends among different industries and communities. Companies can purchase this data to get a better idea about how best to move forward with their operations, whether that be where they should expand, whom they should sell to or what products or services their competitors are using, etc.
- Recruiter – You can probably guess what this one's

for. Recruiters, hiring managers and headhunters will use this tool to search for suitable candidates for whatever role they're trying to fill. These are the people you're trying to stand out to.

- Jobs – This is essentially LinkedIn's own-brand job board. With this, you can apply for jobs directly through LinkedIn without having to go via another website (it's worth noting that if you're using this, whoever sees your application will look at your LinkedIn profile before even glancing at your CV).

So, clearly, it's those last two that we want to focus on. Every bit of information you put into your LinkedIn profile will be able to be used to find you. Therefore, it's vital that the information on that profile is detailed, accurate and geared towards your desired role. There's the old saying, 'Dress for the job you want, not the job you have.' The same goes for your LinkedIn profile. We refer to this as *optimisation*: fine-tuning your profile so that it's best suited to the role you want.

Every single company we've ever worked with has used LinkedIn either to look for candidates or to vet (and possibly disqualify) ones that they're considering, so getting this right is absolutely crucial.

Let's go ahead and get stuck in.

CHAPTER 2

HEAD-TURNING HEADLINES

The first thing to consider is the first bit of text a recruiter will read. Unfortunately, that's your name, and there's not a lot you can do with that. So, we'll move on to the second thing, which is your headline.

In case you're a complete newbie to LinkedIn and don't know what a headline is in this context, it's really just a short sentence that will always appear just under your name. It appears anywhere your name does, whether that's a preview of your profile, on any posts you make, even on comments.

So, given how heavily this bit of text will be associated with your name, you'd be shocked how few job seekers take advantage of it.

When building a new LinkedIn profile, if you tell it

that you're seeking a job, LinkedIn will suggest the line 'Open to New Opportunities', or something similar. While this will communicate that you're looking for a job, it doesn't tell a recruiter anything about you or what jobs you'd be suitable for.

What you want to achieve with your headline is to grab the reader's attention, pique their interest and spark their curiosity. We can give you a simple formula to get you on the right track:

✓ Main Role
✓ Main Problem that You Solve
✓ Key Words

So first we have your 'Main Role'. This can either be your current role or the role you're looking to apply for. This doesn't have to be the actual job title itself but a couple of words describing it. A word of advice to those already employed: if you write down a role entirely different to your current one, your boss might figure out that you're looking for a new job!

The 'Main Problem that You Solve' might sound a bit odd. The reason we say this instead of 'Core Skill' or something similar is because you might be brilliant at something, but a recruiter isn't going to care if they can't see how it will help them. If you're able to translate that skill into something that would solve a company's problem, they'll be more likely to want to talk to you.

'Key Words' should be pretty self-explanatory, but

these are essentially the words that you want to help lead recruiters to your page. They could relate to certain skills, qualifications, experience, brands, software; like a Google search, you want to be able to match as many of a recruiter's search criteria as possible so you appear at the top of their results.

So, for example, you could be someone with video editing experience looking to get into the film industry. Your three sections might be:

- Film editor
- Adept at solving colour grading challenges
- Premiere Pro, After Effects, Movies, TV

The only thing left is to string them all together into prose:

Film editor skilled with Premier Pro and After Effects, solving colour grading challenges across movies and TV.

If you're looking to cast your net a little wider than just one ideal role, pick your favourite and do the above, then add the others afterwards, like this:

Interested in Job Title 1 | Job Title 2 | Job Title 3

After completing your header, take a final look at it to see if you can spice it up with any exciting language. Perhaps instead of 'Interested' you could say 'Fascinated'. Instead of saying you're 'Skilled', consider 'Adept', or that you're 'an Expert in'. It's all about placing yourself miles above anyone that simply says 'Open to New Opportunities'.

As a final note on headlines – and this goes for most of your profile – while using plaintext special characters is fine, steer clear of emojis. More than just looking a bit unprofessional, they're difficult for LinkedIn to index, meaning you'll be harder for recruiters to find.

CHAPTER 3

ALL ABOUT YOU

You might be looking at the 'About' section with a tinge of frustration. *Another chunk of text that I have to write? What do I even put for this?* Don't worry, you don't actually have to write anything new – everything that will go in this section should already be in your CV. Your About section will consist of:

✓ Your Personal Statement

✓ Your Key Achievements

✓ Your Core Skills

✓ Your Education (highest qualification only)

It might seem odd simply copy-and-pasting things from your CV, but in actuality it tends to be a huge pet peeve among recruiters when a candidate's LinkedIn profile doesn't match their CV. If you have identical information in both, it makes it much easier for recruiters to know what's correct.

In terms of how to structure the section, put it in the order given on the previous page. Give each section a heading, except for your personal statement.

For the headings, if you'd like to give them a bit more *oomph*, search 'Unicode Text Converter' on Google. While you can't change fonts within LinkedIn, a unicode text converter will allow you to convert text into a number of different fonts that can be copy-and-pasted over. This way, you can select a bolder font to use for your headlines or to emphasise any key words within the body of the text. Recruiters will know and appreciate the extra bit of effort it will have taken to achieve this. A word of warning, though: don't overdo it, and make sure whatever font you choose is actually legible. Don't make it a chore to read.

At the end of the section, state that you're open to connecting and then include a 'Call to Action' – a simple statement that prompts the reader to do something. In this case, perhaps suggest they message you on LinkedIn or contact you via the 'Contact Details' section.

We *would* suggest putting your contact details, such as email and phone number, directly into the 'About' section, but unfortunately LinkedIn won't like that. Why? Well, as LinkedIn is a business, and makes more money the more time people spend on its platform, it doesn't like it when people share links that will take people *away* from its platform. In terms of the wider effect this has, it means that feed posts with external links to news articles or YouTube videos will be squashed by the algorithm and shown to fewer people. In terms of your 'About' section, even an email address counts as an external link, since clicking it will open your default email app. So, if you include it, your profile will be squashed in the same way a feed post would be. That's why LinkedIn has included a separate section where it allows you to place your contact details. As with many aspects of the internet these days, it's all about appeasing the algorithm.

CHAPTER 4

EXPERIENCE POINTERS

Placing your work history into LinkedIn is fairly simple – as with the 'About' section, it's largely a copy-and-paste job. However, there are a couple of things to help make it airtight.

Firstly, there's your job title. Now, the obvious thing here is to write down whatever your official job title is/was. There are two things to consider here, though. Firstly, if you can match your job title to that of the job advert of your ideal role, then that will mean when recruiters perform their search for candidates, yours will be among the first to pop up. This is because, on the whole, the best candidate for a job is someone who is either already doing it, or has done it in the past. So recruiters will include in their search criteria the job title of whatever role they're looking to fill. Now, we're not telling you to flat out lie – if you don't have the experience, don't pretend you do – but if your role is already close to what the company is looking for, there's no harm in simply matching your job title to theirs.

The only harm there *might* be is if that job title doesn't exist within LinkedIn's records. See, as you type in your job title you'll notice that LinkedIn will try to auto-complete it. If you pick one of these auto-complete options, LinkedIn will be pleased because it will then be able to sort you into whatever categories it likes. If you select something that LinkedIn doesn't recognise, however, then it won't like you very much. It won't be able to sort you, so it will do its level best to ignore you, burying you in the recesses of its database with algorithmic ambivalence.

Therefore, it's a good idea to pick one of the auto-complete options, even if there isn't one that directly matches your job title or that of the job advert. Just pick the closest thing you can find, because that's what the recruiter will do, too.

Next comes the company. Be sure to spell the name of the company exactly right, and if the company has a LinkedIn profile, you should definitely connect with it. This will give your profile much more validity; if someone's profile says they worked at Google, but the Google logo doesn't appear next to it, then the claim seems dubious. It will also make it easier to grow your network if you're connected to the companies you worked with.

For your location, just as with the job title, LinkedIn will prefer it if you let it auto-complete your entry. If you don't, then LinkedIn won't know where you are, meaning it won't be able to include you in searches that use location as a factor. Always do your best to provide ways for LinkedIn to put you in as many of its boxes as possible.

Then you enter the dates. Some people skip this, but it's actually very important, because yet another criterion recruiters can include in their search is the *amount* of experience someone has in a certain role, and this is calculated by looking at these dates. It is in months, however, so don't worry about exact days. If you're still working at the company, be sure to tick the box that says so.

Now we come to the description. Just like with your 'About' section, you are going to copy and paste directly from your CV. Ideally this will then include:
- A short description of the company and your role within it
- Some of your key responsibilities

- The core skills used in the role (and how you used them)
- Your key achievement in the role

If you have copied and pasted, have a quick proof-read to make sure you haven't repeated anything that's already been said earlier in your profile. Also, feel free to edit the formatting, using the unicode text converter where you feel it's appropriate. (A quick tip: some text boxes have a small area at the bottom corner that you can click and drag to make them bigger. This will make it easier to see your formatting in all its glory.)

EDUCATION

We won't give 'Education' its own chapter as it's very similar to 'Experience'. In terms of how much to include, if you've been to university, include your Bachelor's and any qualifications you earned afterwards. If not, just include your highest qualification. Again, when it comes to filling in the fields, let LinkedIn auto-complete as much as it can.

For the 'Activities & Societies' and 'Description' sections, it's up to you how much you write. If you have some professional experience, then recruiters won't really look too hard at your education, so you don't necessarily need to write anything at all. If, however, you're a recent graduate and your degree is your most relevant experience, go ahead and write whatever you think a recruiter will want to read.

For 'Activities & Societies', this means including only those that demonstrate the skills and traits said recruiter will be on the lookout for. You may have been an avid member of the Anime & Manga Society, but that isn't exactly going to help you get a job as a business development manager. That said, if you ended up as a member of a society's committee, then this is worth mentioning regardless of what the society was, since it demonstrates leadership and commitment. Similarly, sports are *always* worth mentioning. Companies lap that stuff right up, seeing it as demonstrative of competitiveness, passion, teamwork and an active mindset. For those of us who are less physically inclined, tough luck.

The 'Description' section, while similar to that of a job role, should not include "responsibilities". If you've been to university, we already know that you had to write essays, give presentations and perform independent research. What we don't know is *what* you wrote/presented/researched. You don't necessarily have to give the title of every one of your essays, but list your key achievements in the form of descriptions of the pieces of work you were particularly proud of and/or received great feedback for.

Within these achievements, ensure you mention the skills you used while achieving them; these are what will matter to recruiters, much more than the specific knowledge you attained.

The strange thing about degrees is that the subject is largely ignored by recruiters: they mostly only care that you *have* a degree, and couldn't care less what it's in. Take us, for example: Matt did Geography at the University of Birmingham and Huw did Drama at Queen Mary University of London. Are either of us working in those fields? No! But, both of us possess the skills that were required to earn those degrees, and those skills (written communication, time management, project management, self-discipline, etc.) tend to extend to most subjects, and happen to transfer quite well into office environments.

CHAPTER 5

JOB-SEEKING ASSETS

Your 'Job-Seeking Assets' are the documents, articles and videos that provide evidence for your skills, experience and expertise. You can place all of these things in the 'Featured' section of your LinkedIn profile.

The one job-seeking asset that everyone will have is their CV. Go ahead and upload this first, giving it the title '[Your Name] CV' so it's nice and simple to see what it is. You can also add a description and, if you like, can add another call to action to prompt recruiters to contact you if they like the look of it.

If you have a video CV (which, if you've read Section 1, you'd know that we recommend), this will be a bit tricky to upload. At the time of writing this book, if you try to upload the video directly to LinkedIn, it decides it doesn't like it. Instead, you have to try a bit of a work-around. We suggest uploading a thumbnail for the video in image form (bonus points if you make it look good), and then add a link to the video within the description (you can host it somewhere like Google Drive or upload it to YouTube as an unlisted video – just make sure the privacy settings are fixed so that anyone with the link can view it).

The more eagle-eyed among you may have noticed that you have the option to add a link directly to the 'Featured' section. Now, as we've said, usually LinkedIn isn't a big fan of external links, but this is an exception as they've provided this space specifically for it. The problem you may run into depends on where you're hosting your video CV. If it's YouTube, then that will be fine, and it will pull through with whatever thumbnail you chose. Videos hosted on Google Drive, however, will pull through with a blank thumbnail, which doesn't inspire much confidence when clicking an unfamiliar link.

If you're a creative and have a portfolio, the Featured section is the perfect place to upload a few examples of your work, so feel free to put your best stuff on there. If there happens to be any online articles written about you recognising some work of yours, go ahead and link them, too.

If there are any documents or articles specific to

roles you've had in the past that you want to show, but not necessarily at the top of your profile, you can add them to sections of your 'Work Experience'. This works exactly the same way as the Featured section. It doesn't just have to be your work, either – if there's a video you watched or an article you read about something to do with the industry that you found interesting, linking these in your job experience will show that you're passionate about your industry. Just make sure not to make it look like you're trying to take credit for someone else's work.

CHAPTER 6

SHOWING SKILLS

We've already said that you should put yourself in as many of LinkedIn's boxes as you can, because that will make it easier for you to show up in the right searches. One of the best ways to do this is with the 'Skills' section. Here's an interesting stat:

- 'Project Managers' we found on LinkedIn within a 50-mile radius of central London: **297,167**
- Those with 'Project Management' listed among their skills: **266,976** (that's **30,191** people who didn't even list their main job role as a skill!)
- Those with 'Project Planning' also listed among their skills: **73,892**, or only **24.9%** of the original number!

So you can see that simply listing *two relevant skills*

can put you ahead of three-quarters of the competition! Imagine what listing three could do! When looking for candidates, recruiters build complex Boolean searches to try to narrow down the pool as much as possible. If you're unaware of what a Boolean search is, aside from being one of our favourite words, a Boolean expression is a query given to a computer that will return either a true or false response. Within this expression you can include the words AND, OR and NOT so that you can add to and exclude certain terms.

This method works on Google. If you want to find web pages relating to penguins, but not emperor penguins, you could search ["penguins", NOT "emperor"]. This will return pages that mention penguins, but filter out any that mention the word "emperor". Similarly, searching ["The Grand Canyon" OR "Mount Everest"] will return pages that mention either of those two things, and ["The Grand Canyon" AND "Mount Everest"] will *only* bring back pages that mention both.

Boolean searches get much more complex than that, but for the purposes of this book, that's all you need to know. Recruiters use Boolean searches to filter candidates based on their experience, qualifications, location, etc. So they might look for software developers OR software engineers, who live in the UK but NOT London, who have five years' experience AND worked at Google. And so on.

A huge part of a recruiter's Boolean search is skills. This is what's going to cut down that huge pool of candidates to a much more manageable number, and you need to make sure that you make the cut.

You have 50 slots for your skills, and we recommend using *all of them* to give yourself the best chance of showing up in searches. You may think it will be difficult to come up with 50 different skills, but remember that many of them are just going to be different wordings and variations of each other ('Presentation' and 'Public Speaking' for example). A good exercise is to take a look at the skills in your CV and, for each one, try to come up with as many ways of wording it as possible. As with other sections, remember only to choose skills that are listed within LinkedIn's system, as these are the ones recruiters will be using in their search.

Finally, don't make the same mistake 30,191 'Project Managers' did: list your main job role as a skill!

CHAPTER 7

FACE VALUE

Earlier we mentioned the different jobs the various social media networks have. When it comes to profile pictures for these networks, the same thing applies. Facebook requires a picture your nan would like, Instagram a picture your friends would like, and Tinder a picture an attractive stranger would like. With LinkedIn, it's a picture your boss would like.

Despite this, you shouldn't worry too much about your LinkedIn photo. It essentially needs to fill two requirements:

✓ Your face is clearly visible

✓ The photo is *appropriate*

Of course, it's that second point that presents the difficulty. What's deemed 'appropriate'? A few things should be obvious, but we'll list them anyway:

- ✖ No visible alcohol/cigarettes
- ✖ No swimwear/shirtless pictures
- ✖ No night-out photos
- ✖ No heavily edited/filtered photos
- ✖ No figurative 'mugshots'
- ✖ No literal mugshots

Other than that, it's really up to you. A good rule of thumb is this: If you were to have a video interview with your ideal company tomorrow, how would you present yourself? Some tips:

- ✓ Check the profile pictures of others in the industry – this will guide you on what to wear
- ✓ Get some good lighting – lamps are your low-budget best friends
- ✓ Be the only one in the photo
- ✓ Have a simple background with maybe a splash of colour to make you stand out
- ✓ Feature just head and shoulders – no one really cares about the rest of your body
- ✓ Smile – sounds corny, but you have *no idea* how huge an effect it has on building trust, familiarity and likeability

With your profile picture taken, the next step is your banner.

BANNER

The banner photo presents a bit of a mystery for most, with many choosing simply to leave it as the default option. As you could probably guess, we don't recommend this. Your banner is some prime real estate that can go a long way to establishing a first impression. With your banner, you can state right off the bat:

✓ Your ideal position
✓ Your contact details
✓ A core skill or two

If you happen to be a whiz in Photoshop or a similar software, you can go ahead and mock something up yourself, paying attention to LinkedIn's banner dimensions.

If you aren't as savvy with that kind of software, don't worry, we have you covered. If you visit **Canva.com**, you'll find a totally free online service that lets you create custom graphics incredibly easily. They have a myriad of different templates for every kind of social media, such as Instagram posts and stories, YouTube thumbnails, Facebook cover photos, the works. Most importantly for us, however, is that they have a ton of templates for LinkedIn banners. Go ahead and scroll through to find one that you like, and then edit it to pop your own details in. After that, save it and upload it to LinkedIn, and there you go: you've got a profes-sional-looking banner without having spent a penny. Easy as pie.

CHAPTER 8

OPTIMISATION HACKS

By this point, your profile should already have reached All-Star status. There are still a couple of 'hacks' we can perform to tighten some nuts and bolts and get it in the best shape possible.

The first 'hack' is your URL: the string of letters and numbers that if entered after *linkedin.com/in/* will lead people to your profile. Did you know that you can edit this? If you go to your profile and look at the right-hand side, you should see a button that says 'Edit Public Profile and URL'. From there, you should be able to see the option to edit your URL. This is where those with unique names will have the biggest advantage, because the likelihood will be that you can simply enter your name and have that be your URL.

If, however, your name is John Smith, then this becomes a little more difficult. Try to get as close to your name as possible, but, failing that, you could consider adding things like middle names, your home town, your job title, or any other identifiers. (While you're in this section, be sure to check that your profile is public so that recruiters can actually find you!)

Having a simple and memorable URL won't necessarily be the factor that gets you a job interview, but it's one of the small things that can really add to a recruiter's first impression.

Next comes your network. It's tempting only to connect with your friends, just as with any other social media, but on LinkedIn you want to try to grow it as much as possible. On the home page, you should see a prompt that says 'Grow Your Network'. Click this and connect with as many relevant people as you can find. This will give you much more visibility in the algorithm.

Incidentally, if you'd like to connect with either of us then you are absolutely welcome to. Our URLs are:

Matt: *linkedin.com/in/mattsedgwick/*

Huw: *linkedin.com/in/huw-landauer/*

(Notice how we both managed to get just our names?)

The next 'hack' is a very simple one. Next to the 'Grow Your Network' prompt, you should also see one that suggests you set up a job alert. All you need to do is pop in your ideal job title and your location, and LinkedIn will begin to notify you when jobs with that title in that location become available.

After that, we'll look at your contact information. We've stated before, but will reiterate now, that you should not list contact details in any other sections or in your posts since LinkedIn will see them as external links. Instead, refer them to your Contact Info section. Here you can place whatever details you'd like, but we'd recommend at the very least an email address and phone number.* As with your CV, please use a simple and appropriate email address, and not the one you made when you were 12.

Did you know that you can create a second profile in a different language? Right under the 'Public Profile and URL' button you'll find the option to 'Add a Profile in Another Language'. This is great for those who are multilingual or are targeting certain parts of the world. Even if you don't speak another language and are happy where you are, it's nice to do this just to show LinkedIn that you know how!

The final 'hack' we'll talk about is the option to state that you're open to work. Of course, this is vital for a

*You can, if you like, place your contact details in your banner. Since this is an image, LinkedIn won't be able to read the text and so won't count anything in there as a link.

job-seeker, as it's something that recruiters will often include in their Boolean search to narrow down their pool of candidates. All you need to do is click on 'Add Profile Section', then go to 'Intro' and click on 'Looking for a New Job'. From here you'll be able to add the job titles you're interested in, the locations you're open to working in, whether you want to start immediately or can afford to wait a while, and what type of job (full-time, part-time, casual etc.) you want. You can then also choose who can see that you're looking for a job: everyone, or just recruiters using LinkedIn's recruiting tool. If you choose the 'everyone' option, this will add a frame to your profile picture that identifies you as 'Open to Work'. If, however, you already have a job and don't want your colleagues seeing that you're looking for something new, just pick the 'Recruiters Only' option. *But the hiring manager at my work uses LinkedIn Recruiter! What if they see me?* Don't worry too much. LinkedIn does a pretty good job of hiding your job-seeking status from people who work at the same place as you. As long as you both have it listed as your current company, you'll be hidden from their view.

CHAPTER 9

CONCLUSION

By following all the advice in this section, you will be placing yourself light-years ahead of most of the competition. You'll notice that none of the things we've recommended are even that difficult – hell, even the written sections are largely copy-and-pasted from your CV. The difference is not that these things are hard, just that most simply *don't do them at all*.

As this section has been about your LinkedIn *profile*, we've not talked at all about engagement such as messages, posts and comments. We'll be talking more about these things in Section 3: **Engaging With Your Future Employer**, but for now we'll give you a couple of quick tips:

- Engage often, reacting to and commenting on posts. This will increase your visibility.
- Make posts when you have something to say about the industry, and every now and then you can talk about your own work. Don't speak about yourself all the time, though, as it will come across as braggy and self-centred.
- Share and comment on articles you find interesting. If the article is hosted somewhere other than LinkedIn, however, add the link in the comments rather than the post. Remember, LinkedIn doesn't like external links.
- Don't be afraid to connect with strangers – the worst they can do is say no.

And that's it! We'll leave you with some screenshots of the profile Matt created while we were producing the **Udemy** course on which we based this book; we would show our actual profiles, but given that neither of us is actively job-searching right now, those profiles don't consist of the same things that yours should.

MATT'S JOB-SEEKING PROFILE

Matt Sedgwick
Talent Acquisition Partner
matt@keyfocusconsulting.com
07552 123 456

Add profile section ▼   More...

Matt Sedgwick

Talent Acquistion Partner passionate about helping Start-Up & High Growth businesses save money, whilst recruiting exceptional talent. Interested in Talent Acquistion Partner | Head of Recruitment | Recruitment Director

Borehamwood, England, United Kingdom · Contact info

Key Focus Consulting
University of Birmingham

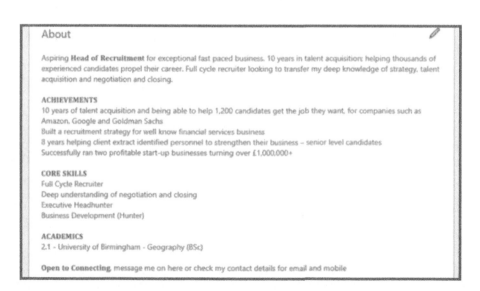

About

Aspiring **Head of Recruitment** for exceptional fast paced business. 10 years in talent acquisition; helping thousands of experienced candidates propel their career. Full cycle recruiter looking to transfer my deep knowledge of strategy, talent acquisition and negotiation and closing.

ACHIEVEMENTS
10 years of talent acquisition and being able to help 1,200 candidates get the job they want, for companies such as Amazon, Google and Goldman Sachs
Built a recruitment strategy for well know financial services business
8 years helping client extract identified personnel to strengthen their business – senior level candidates
Successfully ran two profitable start-up businesses turning over £1,000,000+

CORE SKILLS
Full Cycle Recruiter
Deep understanding of negotiation and closing
Executive Headhunter
Business Development (Hunter)

ACADEMICS
2.1 - University of Birmingham - Geography (BSc)

Open to Connecting, message me on here or check my contact details for email and mobile

Featured $+$ ✏

Dont be afraid to say hello

Click here to see my video CV -
https://drive.google.com/file/d/1zci9iGNmXz9ieB25o...

Matt Sedgwick CV

CV for hiring managers and recruiters. Feel free to
contact me

Experience $+$ ✏

Talent Acquisition Lead
Key Focus Consulting · Full-time
Jan 2019 – Present · 1 yr 8 mos
London, England, United Kingdom

A full spectrum sales talent management consultancy, who build recruitment strategies for SMEs and recruit them top performing talent using their talent attraction and talent acquisition methodology. Mission: 'Reduce Clients' Recruitment Spend'. Revenue from £0 to £500,000 in year one.

Full Cycle Recruitment – engaged with key clients (including Foresight Group, Cognism and Arthur Online) to help them identify and headhunt specific sales talent. Full cycle process from intelligence and research to negotiating and closing.

Strategy Creation – built and executed strategy for high growth businesses. Placed onsite to ensure successful execution. Implemented skill gap analysis, psychometric testing, and highly effective interview coaching. Provided shareholders with reports and data analysis to show effectiveness of strategy.

Team Management – responsible for nine members of staff. Accountable for their onboarding, training and development, motivation, week success cadences and monthly appraisals.
Adapted to Start Up Environment – highly adaptable to ensure successful growth of the business. Created start-up culture from day one that abled staff to understand vision and mission and growth plans of the business.

Stakeholder Management – constantly managed internal stakeholders successfully to ensure cohesion of the business. Worked closely with external stakeholders to deliver high quality services in a friendly, transparent manner.

Key Achievement: Successfully recruited senior member of staff for....... equating to..... in revenue for Key Focus Consulting

see less

Education $+$ ✏

University of Birmingham
Bacnelor of Science - BS, Geography, 2.1
2007 – 2010

SECTION THREE

ENGAGING WITH YOUR FUTURE EMPLOYER

CHAPTER 1

BIT OF A BORING TITLE ISN'T IT?

We know. Unfortunately, this happens to be one of those topics that is difficult to sum up in a neat little headline. It's not as simple as 'Talking to People' or 'Writing a Cool Covering Letter' or 'Looking Good Online'. It's personal to you, and it incorporates not only who you are, but who you're trying to impress.

So the first question that's probably come to mind is *What do you mean by 'engagement'?* It's a good question, too. And no, we're not telling you to ask your future boss to run away with you to Vegas and elope.

Engagement, in our terms, is essentially everything that you do to interact with your future employer (other than by sending them your CV) before you go to interview. This includes messaging them on LinkedIn, email communications, sending your covering letter and any short phone calls you might have (excluding phone/video interviews, which we will cover in Section 4: **Winning In Interviews**).

When it comes to communication like this, many candidates find themselves at a bit of a dead-end. What you say, how you say it, when you say it, where you say it (email, LinkedIn, etc.), and even who you say it to all come into question, which can sometimes, understandably, become a little overwhelming.

Over the course of this section, we'll endeavour to dispel some of this confusion and make this communication much easier. There are, however, a couple of things to sort out before you even know who it is you'll be communicating with.

CHAPTER 2

REPAIRING YOUR DIGITAL REP

Digital reputation is better understood within the context of companies. The phrase refers to how a business presents and frames itself online, affecting how the company is seen as a whole. This means its website, its LinkedIn page, Facebook, Twitter, Instagram, even the way it communicates through email. Anything pertaining to the company that's seen online contributes to its digital reputation.

You might notice, then, that this means a company's digital reputation isn't entirely under its control. Any reviews, photos, articles, tweets or posts about the company written by *anyone else* also factor into this reputation. In fact, even the absence of a response to one of these things will affect it.

For example, let's say a huge fast food-chain, let's call them... oh, I don't know... Mississippi Roasted Turkey, have an excellent online presence. They try really hard to present themselves on Twitter as down to earth and 'with it' (to use a phrase that no one who is 'with it' ever actually uses). They post memes, have banter with other brand social accounts, and even post about ending systemic injustice and fighting climate change.

One day, however, a video surfaces from inside MRT's turkey farms, revealing that MRT do not use turkeys in their food, opting instead for an endangered species of pygmy ostrich. **#MRO** and **#OstrichGate** are suddenly trending, and people everywhere are hounding MRT for a response to the video.

They never respond.

After that, no matter how much MRT try to claw back their reputation, no number of memes can salvage the mess made by OstrichGate. Whenever someone looks into the company, all they find is the news story that the company failed to acknowledge.

The existence of the video was not within their control, but their *response* to it was.

What has this got to do with me? Well, companies aren't the only ones with digital reputations. Individuals have them, too, and by individuals, yes, we mean you. That means everything you do online impacts how you will be seen by other people and, most importantly, by potential employers. That's *everything*, by the way, even the Twitter account you haven't used since 2014.

Before a recruiter or hiring manager even considers you a candidate, they will look you up on Google. It's a classic 'nothing to hide, nothing to fear' situation; if you've got a squeaky-clean record, recently purged any unsavoury things from your past, locked your privacy settings up tighter than Fort Knox (or somehow *didn't* go through an embarrassing stage in your early twenties during which you collected empty bottles of alcohol so you could show off how cool you were for drinking so much), then you'll probably be fine. If, however, the thought of your future boss scrolling all the way through your Facebook timeline sends figurative fire ants crawling down your spine, it may be worth taking action.

That said, we would generally recommend doing this anyway, because you never know what things you may have tweeted a few years ago that, though fine back then, might under the blinding headlights of hindsight come across as insensitive, ignorant, or just plain idiotic. If you say that you've never said anything stupid, you've already proven yourself wrong.

There are two ways to ensure you can sleep comfortably without memories of your My Chemical Romance phase haunting your dreams:

1. Fix your privacy settings
2. Social media audit

These two methods have different levels of difficulty, but also have different levels of effectiveness.

Fixing your privacy settings is fairly easy. All you need to do is go through all your social media accounts (including the ones you don't use anymore), head into the settings and switch all of them from Public to Private. This, obviously, will mean that if someone hasn't already connected with you, they won't be able to see your content. It's a nice and easy way of hiding all your stuff from potential peekers. There are, however, a couple of drawbacks here.

The first applies if you, as a person, prefer to be more of an open book. Locking all your privacy settings up means that you won't be able to be found by friends of friends or interested strangers – of course, for some this is brilliant, but others prefer to be able to be found.

The second drawback is a little unfair. If you hide all your content, it might result in the suspicion that you are hiding it *for a reason*. Now, this isn't necessarily going to discount you from a role, but if you begin an interview with your interviewer feeling suspicious of you, it's going to be much harder to gain their trust. Trust is incredibly important to the success of an interview, so you want to avoid or somehow dispel this suspicion if you can. The best way to engender trust is to appear transparent, so setting all of your social media to Private is going to work against you.

A social media audit is a much more difficult process, but it's much more effective. What it entails is venturing through the entirety of your social media and manually taking down anything that might hinder your chances with a future employer. As to what this might be, it really depends on your industry and what kind of companies you're looking to work with. You can make an evening of it, though, and play this simple game: every time you cringe, take a shot of your chosen drink. You'll be having fun in no time.

The first thing to remember is to look not only at your own posts, but anything you've been tagged in as well; you don't want an unfortunate drunk photo posted by your best mate to trip you up in your application. The second thing is to check the comments on your posts, too. This is because some companies won't like it if it seems as though you associate with the wrong crowd. We once had a client turn down a candidate because they found a photo of them smoking on Facebook – the smoking was fine, but it was the inappropriate and offensive comments their friends made *beneath* the photo that soured the hiring manager's perception of the candidate. So, make sure you go through your internet past with a fine-tooth comb, sweeping up and disposing of anything that would give an employer any reason to drop your CV into the recycling bin.

Once you're finished either with your privacy settings or your social media audit, the best way to check if your efforts have worked is to do exactly what a recruiter would: google yourself.

Don't just search your name (especially if you have a fairly common one); instead, include any factors that would narrow down the search specifically to you. This could be your hometown, your university, your job title – anything a recruiter would be able to use to find you. Then, simply scroll through the results and see what comes up. Be sure to use a few different search engines and explore image and news searches as well. Turn on private or incognito browsing so that it's not taking into account your previous history to find you relevant results. This way, you'll be able to see exactly what can be found about you.

Once you're happy with which bits of your past can be seen, it's time to turn your attention to the present. Think about your profile pictures, your various bios, and the kind of language you use in your posts. We're not saying you have to slap **GIVE ME A JOB** on everything, but it may be worth steering your 'personal brand' towards something you'd want a potential employer to see. For example, your Twitter bio might feature some sort of nihilistic, self-deprecating or hilariously damning and bleak meme. While a bio like this might speak to your soul, it won't be the sort of thing to inspire confidence in a hiring manager. You want your online presence to project an air of positivity and put-togetherness, because this will serve as an excellent pre-first impression.

Now, you can be sure that when you're seen, it'll be from the best possible angle. The next step is to get yourself seen in the first place.

CHAPTER 3

HOW TO LINK ON LINKEDIN

We know, we know, we just did a whole other section on LinkedIn. However, whereas that was all about setting up your LinkedIn *profile*, this chapter is going to talk about how to *use* it to build your network and talk to people.

BEING ACTIVE

You can think of LinkedIn as being like a massive industry conference that's going on all the time. A lot of people seem to think that if they just turn up in their best business clothes and stand grinning at the side of the room with their CV in their hand, occasionally throwing a thumbs up when they hear something they agree with, someone will notice them and toss them a job. Unfortunately, it doesn't quite work like that. You actually have to make your way around the conference, interacting with people in your industry and discussing trends and events that are occurring in your sphere. It's only by doing this that you'll make any kind of impact and prove that you're someone worth knowing.

If it wasn't clear, we're recommending that you don't just sit on LinkedIn and 'like' a post every so often. Instead, find relevant news to do with your industry and interests and comment on it. Even better, respond to other people's comments and get a conversation going. This is a good way not only to be seen by those specific people, but to get elevated in the eyes of the *all-powerful algorithm*; the more you engage and interact with their platform, the more visibility LinkedIn will give you.

Similarly, don't just 'share' articles without adding anything to the conversation. This is like standing silently in the middle of the conference holding a big sign with an arrow on it pointing to something else in the room. Even if people look at whatever the arrow is pointing to, no one will care who's holding the sign. Instead, add some commentary, give your opinion or share a relevant anecdote. Give people a reason to engage and interact with *you*.

Finally, it's tempting to use LinkedIn as a mouthpiece to talk about how great and successful you are. While there is space for posts that celebrate your work and your achievements, if the only topic you talk about is yourself, you'll come across as narcissistic. Not only that, but it fails to open up the floor to conversation; if someone brags to the room at a party about all the important clients they've worked with, are you more likely to ask them follow-up questions, or creep over to the kitchen and hope they don't address you directly? If you are making a celebratory post about yourself, be sure to end it with a question asking people about their own similar experiences. This way, you're celebrating *with* people, not just *at* them.

NOW YOU'RE TALKING

Once you've explored the conference a bit, sauntering around seminars and lingering in lectures, you may decide it's time to strike up a conversation with someone. The trouble here, of course, is identifying who's worth talking to. You don't want to waste your time chatting to people who aren't in your industry, aren't right for you, or aren't even looking for someone like you. So, how do you narrow things down?

You need to create what's called a company persona. This is essentially a description of your hypothetical ideal company. This is entirely based on you and what you want, so your ideal company's culture, size, location, priorities and progression structure.

The best way to structure your company persona is to ask yourself these questions:

1. What's my ideal **job title**?
2. Who would I **report to**?
3. What **industry** do I want to work in?
4. What's my ideal **company culture**?
5. What's my ideal company **size** (number of employees, e.g. under 50)
6. What's my ideal **location**?

Feel free to add any more important information. When you have this, you can use it to search for companies on LinkedIn that fit the description. After that, look in their 'People' section and search for the job title you specified as the one you would ideally report to. If there's no one matching this exact description, find someone that's as close to it as possible. This is your first target.

SPEAKING THEIR LANGUAGE

Now comes the all-important opening message. If the empty box and blinking cursor cause you to stop in your tracks, don't worry: this hurdle is one that most people find tricky to vault. You want to catch their attention, but for the right reasons. You want to give them enough information without rambling on at them. You want to encourage a response without coming off as needy and cloying. So, how do you do it?

In order to communicate with someone in their language and have a meaningful first connection, we need to utilise:

- Triggers
- Priorities

We're sure you don't need us to define the word 'trigger', but in this context we're referring to a particular event or circumstance within a company or its industry that *triggers* something else. Some examples of this might be:

- An economic downturn, forcing it to come up with cost-cutting solutions
- Company growth, providing it with the opportunity to expand into new areas
- Winning an award, giving it some good press and, therefore, more business
- Merging with another company, making it reorganise the structure of the business

Triggers like this are great jumping-off points; referencing a recent one in your message shows that you have done your research and are not just sending the same message to everyone. It also creates a sense of urgency in the suggestion of cause and effect: 'That has happened, so you must *react* with this'. What you need to do here is create pain. It sounds harsh, but we're not talking about insulting or harming them. No, what we mean is that you need to bring a problem to their attention, purely so that you can offer to swoop in and solve it.

In order to know what problem will matter to them, however, you need to know what their priorities are. This can depend on the trigger itself: if there's been an economic downturn, their priority might be stabilising their budget. Sometimes, the priority will depend on the position of the person you're messaging: if they're in human resources, their priority might be mass hiring or diversifying the team's skillset. All it takes is a quick bout of research into the recipient of your message and their company to find out what is currently important to them. This way, when you try to create pain, you can make sure you hit a nerve.

AIDA

Who's Aida? Not 'who', but 'what'. AIDA is a technique used by salespeople to construct pitches to potential clients, and by marketers and copywriters to create engaging advertisements. We're going to use it here because what you're doing is essentially pitching and advertising yourself to this potential employer. AIDA stands for:

- Attention
- Interest
- Desire
- Action

These are the four stages your message should follow: first, get your recipient's attention, then spark their interest, offer something they desire, and then encourage them to take action.

Let's imagine that the person you're messaging is the head of recruitment at a technology company that's going through a merger, and their priority is creating stability within the organisation. Let's say you are someone with experience in managing people within this industry. We'll take this message step by step and walk you through how we would craft it.

Attention: *Can you believe the SaaS market is now worth $157 billion?*

We always like to start with a question, even a rhetorical one, because a question automatically demands an answer. Something like this, which not only references the industry but shows you know your stuff about it, too, can really grab their attention.

Interest: *After your recent merger with TechCorp, you now make up 2.5% of that figure! Such a leap in power also comes with a considerable hop in responsibility, and managing a team of professionals through a transitional time like this is just another huge task to add to your ever-increasing stock of spinning plates.*

Here, we've introduced that trigger and flaunted another piece of research in the form of that percentage. That's when we bring the pain and pluck the nerve of increased responsibility; more responsibility means more stress, a button we've pressed with the spinning plates imagery.

Desire: *With over 10 years' experience in management, and more than half of that in the technology sector, I know exactly what makes tech teams tick. I specialise in creating solutions to logistical problems such as workflow, scheduling and project management.*

Now we sell. Obviously you don't want to overdo it and come off as bragging, but this is your chance to demonstrate your worth and show that you can be a valuable asset to the business.

Action: *I want to place myself in your network and on your radar. If there's any interest, do let me know, and I'll send through my details or make some time for a short call to discuss possibilities.*

This call to action, or CTA, doesn't need to be very long, it just needs to give your recipient a next step should they be interested. Be careful not to come off as pushy (no 'Connect NOW!' or anything like that), as people generally don't like being told what to do. You may notice that in our message we placed most of the action on ourselves in sending through details or making time for a call. This is because we want to show that we're willing to do the legwork and make sacrifices for the chance to speak. It also takes the work off of their shoulders so that, essentially, all they have to do is say, 'Yes'. We also left the topic of the conversation vague; you don't want to charge in with a, 'So if that sounds good, let's discuss salary and benefits'. Your recipient will be less likely to engage if they feel that by doing so they'll be trapped in a deal – a good conversation never began with one person cornering the other.

Finally, you need to sign off your message with a typical 'Best, Matt'/'Warm regards, Huw', or something similar. Afterwards, consider linking to a relevant blog post or article that your recipient might find interesting. It's another way to demonstrate your research and serves as a good conversation starter.

If you follow all these steps as closely as you can manage, you'll end up with a message that is much easier for the recipient to engage with and respond to. That's not to say that you're guaranteed a job, or even a reply, but you'll have given yourself a much better chance than if you'd just said a simple 'Hi!'

Lastly, we'll just run through a few simple things you can do to really hone your engagement on LinkedIn.

FINAL CHECKLIST

✓ Add relevant people regularly and consistently to build your network. Set a daily target of between five and ten.

✓ In your posts, use three hashtags. LinkedIn likes hashtags, but it doesn't *love* them, so don't overdo it.

✓ Connect with people who use similar hashtags to you in their posts. This keeps your network relevant.

✓ Start conversations rather than just make comments. Keep your contributions open by asking open-ended questions.

✓ Ask thought-provoking questions and send relevant articles to people through the messenger function. It's a good way to create more meaningful connections.

✓ Follow companies instead of just people to increase your 'interests'. This will be good for your profile, algorithmically speaking.

✓ Ask for recommendations and endorsements. This will sky-rocket your profile's validity.

✓ Use Owler to keep yourself informed of relevant updates. It's a tool that keeps track of online activity.

CHAPTER 4

COVERING LETTERS, COVERED

Do I really need a covering letter? We know that in this day and age covering letters can seem a little extraneous and unnecessary (like the word 'extraneous'), and may be a little overly traditional. However, a really nice covering letter is going to be able to do things for you that your CV alone cannot. For this reason, we always recommend sending a covering letter along with any job application you actually care about.

So what are these things that a covering letter can achieve? Well, the first way it can help is to explain and overcome any glaring issues that might arise from your CV, or anything that may be used as a reason to discount you. This could be something like a mysterious gap in your working history, a suspiciously short stint at a company, or a majority of experience in a completely different industry. These things on their own are not a problem; you may have gone travelling, the company may have had to make unexpected lay-offs, or you may only recently have discovered your true calling. The problem arises when a recruiter or hiring manager has to consider the possibility that you were just lazy or bored, or were fired. Sending a covering letter allows you the opportunity to put their mind at ease by giving them the proper context.

The second thing a covering letter does is act as an asset that grabs attention. Not everyone is going to send a covering letter, so the mere act of doing so is already going to make you stand out much more than if you send just a CV. More than just making you stand out, it does so for the right reasons. Writing a covering letter demonstrates that you care about your application, and that you have taken the time to do it properly. The better written and researched your covering letter, the better the impression the recipient will have of you, and the further ahead of the other applicants you will be.

Lastly, it increases familiarity with your recipient, making you more than just a name at the top of a list of skills and experience. It's not going to do as much as can be done with, say, a video CV, but it does allow you to inject some more of your personality. Familiarity is absolutely vital, because we as people are biased towards those with whom we're familiar; familiarity breeds trust, and the more you trust someone, the more likely you are to hire them over someone else.

That said, we realise that the prospect of writing a shiny new covering letter for every single job application you make may be a little overwhelming, so we're going to walk you through building a template that will make the whole process much easier.

QUICK TIPS

First, we'll talk through a few small things to make sure your covering letter is in the best shape.

Don't just replicate your CV. A recruiter or hiring manager is not going to appreciate being made to read the same thing twice, and will hold it against you. Instead, a covering letter should *supplement* your CV, adding context and elaboration where necessary.

Tailor it to the specific organisation. While we do recommend templating your covering letter, simply switching the name at the top before you send it off is going to stick out to any reader as lazy and impersonal. Keep the structure, but make sure to change the language so that it is specific to the company and the job description.

Proofread your letter. Don't rely on Word's spelling and grammar check. Print out your covering letter and take the time to read it out loud. This will prevent you from skimming over any mistakes and will make any awkward language obvious. Consider handing it to someone else to read, too.

Use nice, simple formatting. You shouldn't employ any silly fonts or a rainbow of colours, but at the same time try not to have one solid sleeping pill of 12pt Times New Roman. We recommend using the same style as your CV for the sake of consistency, and be sure to space it well so that it's legible.

Identify your USPs. These are your unique selling points, and are what's going to differentiate you from the rest of the pack. Be positive and confident about what more you have to offer than what's requested in the job description, and why you're the perfect candidate for the job.

Include examples. If you make a claim about your experience or skills, make sure you back it up with some evidence. Otherwise, an employer might think you're just saying what they want to hear.

STRUCTURE

When it comes to length, your covering letter should be no more than one page long, and in some cases needs only be in the body of an email, rather than its own attached document. The structure should consist of:

1. Addresses: Online or not, this is a letter and should be structured as such. Add your name, your email address, your phone number, the date, and any relevant social media links in the top right. Under that and on the left, you should add the recipient's name, the company name and the company's address, which you should be able to find either on its website (often at the bottom), or on LinkedIn.

2. Your opening statement: This should set out why you're writing the letter (though please don't start it with 'I am writing to you because'; it's unnecessary). Start with the position you're applying for, where you saw it advertised, and when you're available to start.

3. Your suitability: Cover why *you specifically* are suitable for the job. Also talk about what attracted you to this type of work, what interests you about the company and what you think you could bring to it.

4. Your strengths: Highlight your relevant experience and the skills you have that specifically match the job description. Then, talk about any additional skills and how they could contribute to the role.

5. The ending: Close the letter by reiterating your interest in the role and your desire for a personal interview. Mention now if there are any dates that you are unavailable. Finally, thank them for reading it and express that you look forward to their response.

Remember, each of these paragraphs should be no more than two or three sentences long.

RESEARCH

We've referenced throughout this section how important it is to show you've done your research. You might well be asking, then, what research you're supposed to do. What are you supposed to know? To help you out, we've put together this list of questions that you should find out the answers to:

✓ What does the company do?
✓ Who are its competitors?
✓ What's the mission of the business?
✓ What's the vision of the business?
✓ What are the company's values and ethics?
✓ What are the triggers?
✓ What are the hiring manager's priorities?
✓ What pain does this create?

Once you know the answers to those questions, you'll be able to write your letter in the correct tone.

TONE & LANGUAGE

Tone is subjective, and there's no one 'right' voice to write in. It entirely depends on the company to which you're applying. During your research you'll start to get a feel for how they communicate, whether that's on their website or social media. In your covering letter, you should try your best to replicate this tone, leaning a little more to the side of professionalism, if possible. This is because when companies look for new staff, they don't just want to find someone who has the right skills and experience: they want to find someone who is also a *cultural* fit for the business. You have an opportunity in your covering letter to demonstrate that you can fit this requirement.

Related to tone is the type of language you employ. A great trick you can use to make sure you're writing in the company's language is to head to **wordclouds.com** and paste the full job advert into the text box. When it processes, it will give you a word cloud that displays the most commonly used words in the advert: the more frequent the word, the bigger it appears in the cloud. You can then use this to see what the company prioritises and work it into your covering letter.

One more tool you can use is **hemingwayapp.com**. This analyses your language and highlights instances of needlessly complex sentences, use of the passive voice, unnecessary adverbs and other common writing errors. Simply pop your covering letter into the system and see what it suggests (but don't take its word as gospel; if you prefer a sentence as is, don't feel you have to change it just because the app tells you to).

Finally, just as with your CV, make sure to insert

brand names, facts and figures wherever you can. These will add validity to your statements and ground them in reality, rather than seeming like you're pulling them from thin air.

SAVE AND SIGN

When it comes to closing your covering letter, give a standard sign-off such as 'Best regards', 'Warm regards', any kind of 'regards', really. Under that, place an electronic signature. This can be done a few different ways, either by scanning a physical signature and placing it in, using Adobe Reader's Fill and Sign feature or even drawing a signature in Microsoft Paint. However you do it, adding a signature is a brilliant way to add a touch of class to your covering letter and show you've made the effort to present it well.

Finally, you need to save your covering letter. Export it as a PDF rather than as a Word file, simply because it's more professional. Don't name it 'Covering Letter' or '[Your Name] Covering Letter'; instead, name it 'FAO [Name of Recipient]' (FAO stands for For the Attention Of). This tells the recipient that the file is specifically for them and will spark their attention. If you just call it 'covering letter', they're likely to switch off immediately.

FINAL CHECKLIST

1. Does your covering letter include all essential information?
   - ✓ Full name
   - ✓ Professional email address
   - ✓ Phone number
   - ✓ Date
   - ✓ Relevant social media profile/s
2. Have you addressed it to the right person?
   - ✓ Hiring manager, or
   - ✓ Your future direct supervisor
3. Does your introductory paragraph grab the reader's attention?
   - ✓ Mentions two or three of your top achievements
   - ✓ Backs up claims with facts and figures
4. Have you explained your suitability for the advertised role?
   - ✓ Identified the job requirements
   - ✓ Demonstrated how you match these requirements
5. Have you communicated your passion for the company?
   - ✓ Listed your three favourite things about the company
   - ✓ Avoided generic reasons for liking the company

6. Have you closed the letter with a good call to action?
    - ✓ Asked for interest, not time
    - ✓ Made it easy to say 'Yes'
7. Did you close the letter formally?
    - ✓ Used a standard sign-off
    - ✓ Added your signature

With that, your covering letter should be absolutely airtight and ready to send to your recipient.

CHAPTER 5

FINAL STEPS

Between sending off your covering letter and being invited to interview, there might be a couple of emails or even a phone call or two between you and your future employer. These might seem scary, but you shouldn't overthink these communications, stressing yourself out and alienating the hiring manager or recruiter. So instead of another *dos* and *don't*s list, we've boiled down our advice into three simple points.

MIRROR THEIR TONE

As for mirroring the tone, this is similar to what we said about covering letters: companies are looking for those who match their culture as well as for people with the required skills and experience. Following a similar tone to theirs in communication indicates you fit that cultural requirement. We're not saying you should change your entire personality (because if you have to in order to fit in, the company isn't right for you), just that you should follow their lead. A small caveat is to be careful when it comes to companies who use relaxed and casual communication styles. Don't let yourself get so comfortable that you slip into using swear words or other entirely inappropriate language – remember that you're still trying to look employable. And yes, that still applies even if *they* swear. All you're trying to do is show that you can operate on the same wavelength.

BE HONEST

Being honest is pretty self-explanatory in that you shouldn't lie about your skills or experience, but it does go a little further. For example, if they ask you whether you're comfortable with a certain aspect of the job that you were unaware of, and you aren't, don't pretend that you are just because you want the job. Ultimately, this will make things difficult both for you and for the company, and it's much more beneficial for both of you if you are honest about your discomfort.

This way, either you can work out a compromise, or you can move on to something better suited to you. You have to think about Future You's happiness, as well as the happiness of Present You.

BE PREPARED

Being prepared simply means that you should know the answer to whatever introductory questions they may ask you over the phone or through email. This could be about references, start dates, availability for interview, or questions regarding your CV or covering letter. You don't want to be left frantically looking through your notes and calendar apps while someone's patiently waiting on the other end of the phone; it looks unprofessional and will lose you points.

And, that's all we have to say on the subject! The last piece of advice is to always 'Remember the Human'; every piece of communication you send has a person on the other end. On the one hand, this means you need to be mindful of being respectful and considerate; on the other, it means allowing yourself to relax a little. They are not a robot, so you shouldn't speak to them like one. Feel free to develop a rapport – this will give you a good head start for the interview.

CHAPTER 6

CONCLUSION

Making contact with a future employer is the last step in the job-search process that is entirely within your control, having 'til now all depended on the assets you create and the way you present yourself and your history. It is simultaneously the *first* step in which you directly interact with someone else, and this transitional period can be very stressful. We hope that in this section we've been able help you navigate these murky waters with a little more confidence.

With that, you should be prepared for every step in the job-search process, right up until the interview. Interviews are arguably the scariest part of the job search process, so we hope you look forward to joining us in Section 4: **Winning in Interviews**!

SECTION FOUR

WINNING IN INTERVIEWS

CHAPTER 1

GETTING INTO INTERVIEWS

Now it says here on your CV that you began your last role in May of 2013, but our investigative team found that it was, in fact, June the second! What do you have to say for yourself, you filthy scoundrel?

This is the sort of question that echoes in our heads as we wake up in a cold sweat the night before a job interview. This is because many people seem to get the word 'interview' confused with the word 'interrogation'. They fear that their interviewer is out to get them: to catch them out and to push the big red button hidden beneath the desk that summons two burly security guards to toss them out of the fifth-floor window.

It only takes a few seconds of looking at interviews

from the interviewer's perspective to realise how ridiculous this is. Firstly, the company already *want* to hire you. If they wanted just to throw out your application, they already would have. The purpose of the interview is to see if there are any glaring red flags that they should consider before hiring you, and to see if your personality matches the culture of their business. The interviewer will understand that you're human and will not expect you to be perfect (and if they do, then that's a red flag on *their* side that should concern *you*). This leads quite nicely on to our next point.

Interviewers are human, too. Remember this throughout the entire interview process and don't forget to treat them as such. This means allowing for small mistakes and not placing them on some distant pedestal. By all means, be respectful, but if they speak to you in a relaxed tone, you're allowed to respond in kind. In fact, as a general rule, always match the tone that the interviewer uses: if they make a joke, laugh and make another one later; if they are more formal, maybe leave the jokes in your head; if they speak about their personal life, ask them a (non-invasive) follow-up question or tell them about a similar experience you've had recently; if they're strictly business, so are you.

All of this is intended to help you feel less nervous about your interview, but it is important to know that it's fine to be a little nervous (though if you're leaving puddles of sweat everywhere you go, that may be a problem). Nerves about a situation only indicate that you care about its outcome. Similarly, admitting that you're nervous is a strength, not a weakness, as it demonstrates self-awareness and a willingness to admit fallibility. A good interviewer will appreciate this and open with some casual conversation to help you relax.

With that out of the way, we'll start with a simple checklist of *do*s and *don't*s to get you through the interview.

CHAPTER 2

WHAT AND WHAT NOT TO DO

Obviously, we're going to go into a bit more depth during the rest of the section, but we thought it'd be a good idea to begin by laying some things out simply so that you can come back and refer to them later.

DO

- ✓ Research the industry (if unfamiliar), the company and your interviewer
- ✓ Practise interviews with friends and family
- ✓ Plan to arrive 15 minutes early
- ✓ Plan your travel route and allow extra time for traffic or unexpected disruptions

- ✓ Dress according to what your research has suggested is appropriate, erring on the side of formality
- ✓ Take a copy of your CV with you
- ✓ Bring your notes with you, but don't carry them into the room
- ✓ Be friendly and engaging with *everyone* you meet (you never know who will report back about you!)
- ✓ Match your interviewer's tone/body language, *but*
- ✓ Remain authentically *you*
- ✓ Be calm and confident, but not apathetic or arrogant
- ✓ Find something in common with your interviewer
- ✓ Ask questions throughout, including 'Why do you do [...] that way?'
- ✓ Answer questions in detail, explaining the 'why' or the 'how' rather than just the 'what'
- ✓ Back up your claims with facts (brands, names and numbers)
- ✓ Anticipate the interviewer's concerns
- ✓ Be honest and secure in your weaknesses, and explain how you're dealing with/working on them
- ✓ Prepare stories that demonstrate your skills
- ✓ Ask challenging questions at the end
- ✓ Ask for next steps and have closing statements
- ✓ Finish with a thank you
- ✓ Evaluate every interview with what went well, what you struggled with and, from this, what you need to work on

DON'T

- Over-rehearse your answers: you'll come across inauthentic and robotic
- Dress too casually: at the *very least* wear a buttoned-up shirt/blouse with black jeans and smart shoes
- Be late, or blame someone else if you are
- Sit on your phone in the lobby while you wait – strike up a conversation, study your notes or at least read a book
- Be overly familiar or casual in tone
- Swear, even if *they* do
- Bad-mouth your current/previous employer; it will only reflect badly on you
- Say you don't have any questions – even if you say they've already answered the ones you were going to ask, this will only tell them you didn't prepare enough
- Ask questions with the intention of catching the interviewer out or making them seem less smart than you; this will paint you as vindictive and unpleasant
- Use empty clichés like 'I'm a team player' or 'I'd say my biggest weakness is being a perfectionist'; this shows a lack of imagination and preparation
- Disrespect/mock the company to the interviewer

as a way to gain familiarity (sounds silly, but it happens!)

This list contains some general advice for any interview. However, as with any rule, there are exceptions. Take, for example, 'Don't bad-mouth your current/ previous employer'. In an interview, you might specifically be asked to identify a situation where a previous employer may have gone wrong. The purpose of such a question is to see how good you are at finding problems, so if you deny the existence of any by saying your employer never went wrong at all, this wouldn't help you. The difference would be to make sure that you still speak respectfully, never attacking the character of any individual manager/colleague, instead stating simply what you would have done differently and why.

What we're trying to say is that every interview is different, and you need to adapt to the tone and style of the room. That is, if you're both in the same room at all...

CHAPTER 3

PHONE AND VIDEO INTERVIEWS

Phone and video interviews were already on the rise before the Covid-19 pandemic, but have shot up in popularity during and since, for obvious reasons. On the surface, these seem easier than face-to-face interviews: they're less formal with lower pressure. To a certain extent, this is true. There are, however, drawbacks. The more barriers there are between two people, the harder it is for them to communicate. The harder it is to communicate, the less complete a picture they will be able to draw of each other. Incomplete pictures create doubt, and a company is less likely to hire someone about whom they have doubts.

It follows, then, that over these interviews you need to ensure you break down as many of these barriers as you can or, if breaking them down isn't an option, at least try to make them more transparent. Let's begin with phone interviews.

PHONE CALLS

More often than not, a phone interview will be purely introductory, to get to know your background a little and confirm the details of your CV. This doesn't mean, however, that they are unimportant; on the contrary, introductory phone interviews can be one of the biggest hurdles in the interview process. As long as you've been honest in your CV and your application, though, you should be absolutely fine. All you need to do is take the phone call seriously.

There's a chance that you'll be called out of the blue by a recruiter or hiring manager regarding a role that you've applied for. This can be stressful, especially if you're busy. Don't worry, they will always ask if you have time to talk because they understand that you're a human being with a life to live. They won't throw away your CV if you politely tell them that now is not a good time and ask that they call you back later, especially if you specify when you'll be free. If you don't tell them you're busy, and then try your best to rush your way through the conversation so that you can get back to whatever it is you were doing, this will tell them that you don't care all that much about the role.

Before they ask if you have time to talk, they'll identify themselves and the company they work for and then say that the call is regarding a role that you applied for. The correct response here is excitement, not 'Which one?' If you're keeping track of your applications (and, as an aside, you absolutely should), the role they're talking about will become apparent fairly quickly. If the first thing you communicate to them is confusion, this sets you off on the wrong foot.

Your next concern should be making sure that the conversation can be heard clearly at both ends. All this means is trying your best to find somewhere quiet, with good phone service, where you're not going to be interrupted. If this is a problem, it is absolutely fine to say so. If you ask to call them back in five or ten minutes so that you can make sure you're in a better environment, this will tell them that you genuinely value the conversation.

If you decide not to delay the conversation, this is where it's important to be prepared. You will be asked questions about your CV and your background. If you don't know the answers, then you'll risk implying that you threw your CV together without much thought. You'll also need to know the answer to other standard questions like 'Where did you hear about the role?', 'When would you be looking to start?', 'Are you interviewing with any other companies right now?'

These questions aren't intended to test you, they're only there so the company can gather data about their applicants. However, if you don't know the answer, you'll risk seeming like you're not paying much attention to your job search.

Related to this, if you've had the opportunity to prepare for the phone call, whether it's a planned interview or you delayed an impromptu one, then use this opportunity to be ready. Prepare some notes on the company and have your CV in front of you. This way you can ensure you'll be able not only to *answer* questions clearly, confidently and accurately, but to *ask* relevant questions, too. If you're taking the call at home, you can also use this time to make sure anyone you live with knows not to barge into the room asking you why you've left the washing-up in the sink for the third time this week.

You'll likely be given some next steps at the end. They might say you'll get another call in the next couple of weeks, or an email regarding an in-person or video interview. On the off chance that they don't give you a next step, ask for one. A simple 'So what comes next?' is all you need to say. They'll likely tell you to expect another email or phone call within the next couple of days.

Other than that, make sure you follow as many of the *do*s and *don't*s listed in Chapter 2 that apply, and you'll sail through the call.

VIDEO CALLS

Video interviews introduce the element of sight, which is like adding a new dimension to a picture, bringing it from 2D to 3D. Suddenly there's this whole other direction to worry about, on top of what you already had with the phone interview. With this new dimension come new problems but, luckily, these problems are mostly quite easy to solve.

First you need to decide what to wear. On top, as with any interview, it depends on the company. Always avoid going too casual (no hoodies/T-shirts/dinosaur onesies), but if you're taking the interview at home, you'll most likely get away with a nice jumper/shirt/blouse. Obviously, you'll only be seen from the waist up, so for all intents and purposes you could wear a tutu and Crocs and your interviewer would be none the wiser. In fact, if you feel that wearing jogging bottoms or pyjama bottoms is going to help you feel more relaxed and confident, then, by all means, go for it. However, you might find that dressing up in a full smart outfit, right down to the shiny shoes, will help you get into a more professional, businesslike mind-set. Ultimately, it comes down to different strokes for different folks, so do whatever you think will give you the best edge. If you do dress more casually down south, just remember not to stand up halfway through the interview and reveal your curry-stained sweats.

Now comes the question of where you'll be. Obviously, somewhere with a decent Wi-Fi connection is a must – you could be the perfect candidate for a job, but an interviewer won't be able to figure that out if you're stuck buffering every 20 seconds. If this means having to commandeer a room in the house that's next to the Wi-Fi router, we're sure your family/ flatmates will understand. We do also recommend your home rather than a public space (or, if you're insane, your current job), just so that you can be in control of who might enter the frame. For this reason, just like with phone interviews, let any housemates know about the interview. In addition to this, make sure you shut any four-legged friends out of the room – we all love a surprise dog visit on a Zoom call, but it doesn't exactly scream 'professionalism'.

Next, you have to decide what will be behind you. We know it doesn't seem like a big deal, and it isn't really. All you have to do is make sure there's nothing distracting like screens, people or street-facing windows in the frame. Movement distracts the eye, and once the eye's distracted, the ears are soon to follow. Also, if you happen to be in your bedroom, do your best not to include your bed in the shot (especially if it's unmade, or if you have novelty Spider-Man sheets). You can also use this to give yourself a little leg-up in how you present yourself; maybe you could have a smart-looking bookcase behind you or some tasteful art (but no movie/TV/celebrity posters). If you're an artist, it might not hurt to have some of your own art in the background as a talking point! If nothing else, you can't go wrong with a plain coloured wall.

Use a laptop if you can, as opposed to a phone. The bigger your display, the larger the image of your interviewer will be, and the more like a real conversation it'll feel. If you do use a phone, place it on a surface rather than holding it in your hand – it'll be distracting if your camera keeps shaking around, and placing it somewhere means you'll have both hands free for gesticulating.

Any Instagram influencer will tell you that angles are everything. Placing your camera so that it's pointing up your nose may not make you a worse sales manager, but it does mean that your interviewer can see how long it's been since you last used a tissue. Place the camera so that it's angled flatly at eye level. You might have to sit your laptop on a few books, but that's fine.

Make sure you're sufficiently lit (no, we don't mean 2017 slang for 'get a little drunk'). You don't need to invest in an intricate lighting rig, but ensuring your face is clearly visible is an absolute must. We do recommend softer lighting from lamps as opposed to overhead bulbs, but it's not vital.

Similar to the phone interview, you should have in front of you, or in a separate window on your laptop, your CV and some notes about the company and the industry. This is one advantage phone and video interviews have over face-to-face interviews, and you should absolutely take it. All we'd ask is that you don't stare at your notes the entire time, or take three minutes to consult them before answering each question. Use them as a reference, not as a crutch.

Speaking of where to look, it's worth noting that interviewers can tell if you are constantly checking yourself out in the little self-view window. If you can't stop admiring yourself, take away the temptation and turn the self-view off. If your interviewer's image isn't near your camera, make sure to let them know, and look at the camera when answering any questions; even if you're technically looking at the interviewer, it can hinder the conversation if, according to their screen, you're looking somewhere off to the side.

You need to be much more wary of the clarity of your speech during a video interview. This is because, whereas in a face-to-face interview your voice is travelling just from your mouth, through the air, to the interviewer's ears, in a video interview it also has to pass through your microphone, your internet connection, their internet connection, and their speakers or headphones. These technological aspects can risk degrading the resolution of your voice *at each stage* if they are of low quality. You will need to compensate for this by prioritising clarity not only in the way you speak (e.g. volume, diction, pace etc.), but by confirming throughout the interview that your interviewer can hear you properly. This just means asking every now and then 'Did you get all that?' or 'Did I come through OK there?' Similarly, confirm that you have heard what they've said by repeating their questions back to them before you answer (though not necessarily in full). If they ask you for your biggest weakness, start with 'I'd say my biggest weakness is...'. If they ask you where you see yourself in five years' time, begin with 'In five years' time I see myself...' It's simple, but it helps prevent any miscommunication between the two of you.

Finally, while it is more difficult to be late for a video interview, it is by no means impossible. Slow-to-start laptops, trouble opening the video call app, Wi-Fi issues, missing notes – all of these things can mean that your two o'clock call begins at ten past. Just like with a face-to-face interview, plan to be early. The worst-case scenario is that you have to wait in front of your laptop for a few minutes.

PRE-SCREEN

Something that's become common in the recruitment world is a format of video interview known as a pre-screen. Instead of speaking with an actual interviewer, applicants are given a series of written questions, for which they have to record video responses. The precise details of these 'interviews' vary: for some, you get unlimited time to read the question and prepare a response, whereas others give you a limit of 30 seconds or a minute; some let you re-record your responses as many times as you need before you submit them, some give you a set number of tries, while others only give you one shot.

These pre-screens, in our professional opinion, aren't always great – the questions can be unclear, or the time limits can be inappropriately short so that candidates struggle to give a complete answer; also, there's the chance that the candidate will take a perfectly normal stumble over a sentence and be unable to start again. In short, there's much less wiggle room with a pre-screen. Despite the issues, pre-screens are being used more and more frequently in competitive markets due to their ability to speed up the recruitment process. The way to deal with them is to treat them exactly like a normal video interview, but with a couple of differences:

- First, since you don't have another human whose tone you can match, always go in on the side of professionalism – you can ease up in future, more traditional, interviews if the tone is more casual.
- Second, read the instructions carefully – you don't want to end up in a situation where your

first response consisted of you stumbling over a sentence, saying 'Ah f**k, that wasn't very good', and turning off the camera only to find that you just had one chance at recording the response and it sent automatically when you hit 'stop'. If that sounds oddly specific, it's because that *exact* thing happened to Huw during his last job search. Heed our warning and study those instructions.

- Third, use whatever time you are given to prepare your response wisely, writing down notes on what you're going to say. If you're given only 30 seconds, though, don't try to write down your whole answer so you can read it back word for word – instead, just write down the key words to save yourself some time.

CHAPTER 4

RE: RESEARCH

Everyone knows that you need to do your research before your interview. After all, you don't want to end up looking like you just walked in off the street, do you? So, you might end up in the same situation that many job-seekers do: you decide to do some research, setting aside an afternoon to go ahead and dive deep into the company, but five minutes in you've googled the company, read their 'About' page, scrolled aimlessly through the rest of their website and are now stuck. Don't worry, you're not alone.

Your research is not supposed to answer every question you may have about the company, but rather give you questions to ask. If you can't find the company's goals, vision or values, those then become questions you can ask your interviewer. You might worry about being tested on company trivia. In certain competitive markets, this may well happen. They might test you to see if you have done your research, but, if they do, it will very rarely be on anything other than surface-level knowledge you can find on their website. If the year in which they were established can't be found easily either via their website or social media pages, they are not going to ask you about it.

So what *should* your research include? In addition to studying the company's website and social media presence, it's worth broadening the subject to include the entire industry. You should be up to date on the industry's trends at least over the last six months. This will help you ask more insightful, informed questions about how the company reacted to certain events or developments, or how they plan to deal with future circumstances. Look at news websites (there will be sites dedicated to industry news, you just need to look for them) or go directly to the blogs of both the company you're applying to and their competitors to find the most relevant articles.

After this, you need to narrow your search from the industry and the company to your interviewer. Contrary to your (hopefully) natural instincts, stalking your interviewer a little on LinkedIn is absolutely fine. This is because LinkedIn as a social media platform is where people will put the content they *want* their professional network to see. As a potential employee, you are being ushered into that network, so you are well within your boundaries to take a look at their post history. You're not going to find any scandalous family drama or beach holiday photos, just things to do with their professional life. This stuff is perfect to ask questions about. Just don't go investigating their Instagram.

The final thing you should research is yourself. This includes inspecting your work history as it's written in both your LinkedIn profile and your CV, making sure you know what they say and that they say the same thing. It also includes taking some time to google yourself. We spoke about your 'digital reputation' in Section 3, but to sum it up here, your digital reputation refers to how you appear online. If someone were to find all your social media profiles and anything else that exists about you on the internet, what impression of you would they draw? Do you have anything embarrassing or inappropriate that might give a potential employer any concerns? If yes, consider taking some things down or just tightening up your profile's privacy settings.

Once you've completed all your research, you would be forgiven for considering it a good idea to prove it in the interview by asking ultra-specific questions that, rather than being borne out of genuine curiosity, are there purely to demonstrate that you've done your homework. It may be a surprise, but this isn't actually helpful. Interviewers will not be impressed that you've researched the company because they consider it the bare minimum, and if you imply that you think it's deserving of praise, this will give them concern. It's like that one person we all know who goes around bragging about how 'nice' they are – the fact they seem to find common decency difficult enough that they consider it a virtue is worrying, isn't it? It's the same case here.

CHAPTER 5

BETWEEN THE LINES

Let's say your interview is at 2pm. You rock up at 1:45pm, have a chat with the receptionist, and read a book while you wait patiently for your interviewer to arrive. When they do, you stand up, smile and shake their hand. All good so far. Then they ask, *So what have you been up to today?*

You answer, *Well, I got up at about 11am, had a quick shower and then played Animal Crossing until I had to leave to come here.*

While this may well be the truth, it's the wrong answer. When your interviewer asks you this question, even if the tone is casual and you're not even in the interview room yet, they are not just asking out of curiosity. The question they are really asking is,

Do you use your time wisely? They want to know if you've spent the morning productively, using it to prepare for the interview, run errands or work on anything. While your free time is your own and you can use it as you wish, how a person spends their free time says a lot about them, especially the time before an interview. Now, we're not telling you to lie to the interviewer at all, we're advising you to use that time effectively so that the truth looks good. However, this doesn't mean that you can't relax on the morning of your interview if you need to calm your nerves and get in the right headspace; in that case, telling your interviewer that you spent the morning getting ready for the interview would be absolutely true, so go ahead and tell them so.

This applies to similar questions about the weekend, or just 'recently'. When interviewers ask these questions, it's to see if you actually do anything in your spare time, or spend it sitting around staring at screens. You might then ask us, *But what if I DO spend all my time sitting around staring at screens?* In this instance, our advice has nothing to do with the interview; it's simply to get yourself a hobby and make more plans to spend time with friends, and not just in the pub. Not only will this give you a good answer to these questions and make you more employable, it will also make you a more generally interesting person.

Questions with hidden meanings will be dotted all

over the interview. Whether you're being asked what your strengths and weaknesses are, how your 'nemesis' would describe you, or what Pokémon you'd be and why, any seemingly simple question has layers behind it designed to determine who you are, what you can do and what you know about yourself.

Let's take, for example, *What's your biggest weakness?* Now, anyone with half a brain cell knows that *I tend to sabotage any romantic relationship I get into* is not an appropriate answer – it's too personal and has nothing to do with your professional life. Equally, however, *I never know when to give up* or *I just care too much* are wrong answers, too. You often hear the advice to 'turn strengths into weaknesses', with the intent of making interviewers think, *Now wait a minute, we wouldn't consider that a weakness at all, so if that's a weakness to you, then you must be faultless and perfect!*

Let's put aside for the moment the fact that interviewers aren't idiots, are fully aware of this advice, and can smell these answers a mile off. Everyone gets the hidden meaning of this question wrong; they think the hidden meaning is, *Why shouldn't we hire you?* In fact, it's, *Do you have the self-awareness to recognise your own faults, and are you working on them?* Offering these pretend weaknesses is not only brazenly dishonest, it tells the interviewer that you're not secure enough in yourself to own up to your faults. This is an issue because it will be much easier for a manager to prepare for a problem you're aware of than one whose existence you refuse to acknowledge.

You might be wondering what you're supposed to say if you actually are, for example, a perfectionist to a fault. As with any other weakness you might describe, you should follow a simple formula:

1. What it is: *I'm a perfectionist.*
2. How it hinders you: *I sometimes waste time polishing things unnecessarily, ignoring things that might be more important.*
3. How you're working to improve: *I've started setting myself time limits for projects so that I don't waste too much time.*

Following this formula will allow you to be honest about your shortcomings without worrying the interviewer, as you've demonstrated your maturity in your willingness to work on them.

Every time you get asked a question in an interview, pause and consider what the hidden question might be. This will help you to answer the question properly. To assist with this, in Chapter 7 of this section, we've written a list of common interview questions, as well as some of the hidden meanings that might be behind them.

CHAPTER 6

TECHNIQUE

If you've ever been asked to give an example of a time that you showed a certain trait, like out-of-the-box thinking or integrity, you might have responded in a couple of ways. The first way was to stammer and stutter because you didn't know how your shelf-stacking supermarket job could ever have called for integrity.* The second response was to forge ahead and give it your best shot, recounting the time that you refused to give your own mother a discount, even though you had the power, because it was against policy. The beginning of the story went well, and you

*This is extremely common, and it's a result of a lack of preparation. As an exercise, sit down and write a basic answer, or at least a rough outline, for each one of the common questions in the list in Chapter 7.

were somewhere in the middle when you realised you didn't have an ending. Instead, you let the momentum run down until you simply said, *So, yeah, um, I think that showed integrity...* You then looked expectantly at the interviewer, hoping they'd move on to an easier question.

This second response is symptomatic of a lack of technique: while you have a good answer in there somewhere, it gets obscured because you don't know how to articulate it properly. In this chapter, we want to give you a couple of simple techniques to help you construct responses that follow a clear through line and communicate your story effectively.

PEA

We'll start with a simple technique that suits simple questions (although again, always consider the hidden question). You might recognise this technique from English class back in school, since you were probably taught it in reference to writing analytical paragraphs. The formula is:

Point

Explain

Apply

Are memories of *To Kill a Mockingbird* or *Much Ado About Nothing* starting to flood back into your head?

If so, we dearly apologise. You may remember it this way, or perhaps E and A stood for 'Evidence' and 'Analyse'. Regardless, we'll run through this technique with a demonstration. Let's say the question here was *What motivates you?*

First, we need to make our point. For the purpose of this demonstration we'll say that self-improvement is what motivates you. In this case, the beginning of your answer could be, *I'm incredibly motivated by self-improvement, whether that's in terms of my skills, my lifestyle or my knowledge.*

A lot of people would stop here, because they think they've answered the question. The trouble is that the interviewer has nothing but your word to go on. You need to explain how you know this. In this example, you might say, *During the period I've been looking for work, I've had a lot more free time, which I've spent teaching myself how to draw. While I had no skill at all to start with, I've now reached a point where if I have something in my head I can at least put it to paper recognisably. Doing this has helped me to feel productive and made it so that I feel that I'm using this time effectively.*

The last step is to bring your answer back round to the context of the interview and apply it to the role. So it could be, *I think this will really come in useful in this role, since I know it involves constantly learning new things and developing new skills.*

Giving an answer like this tells the interviewer much more about you than if you just said 'Success' or 'Money', and also shows that you know yourself very well. Remember, this interviewer has asked about your motivations because they want to know if what they have to offer will be enough to motivate you in your role, or if you'll end up bored and disinterested. This technique will work for anything that's a simple question and answer. For more complex, open-ended questions like the ones we talked about at the start of the chapter, it's better to use the next technique.

STARR

Some questions will require you to tell a story in response. For these, the **PEA** method won't fit. You'll have to use a technique that makes sure you can communicate the story clearly and effectively, hitting all the points you need to hit while staying on one coherent track. That's where the **STARR** technique comes in.

Situation

Task

Action

Result

Reflect

For this example, let's use the question *Could you give an example of when you thought outside the box?*

We'll pretend that you used to be a teacher's assistant.

Your first job is to lay out the context, or the situation: *I was assisting a Year 9 English class at a historically rough school.*

Then you describe the task, problem, or challenge you were facing: *At this school, any time poetry came around in the syllabus, many male students would refuse to try because they were afraid of looking feminine.*

Next, tell the interviewer what action you took: *Before, teachers had unsuccessfully offered prizes for the 'best' poem. I instead suggested offering a prize for the 'cheesiest'.*

After that, recount the results of your actions: *While a couple of students still refused to participate, there were a few who got very excited about it and produced some surprisingly impressive poetry. As a plus, they also volunteered to read their poems out loud to the class, which ended up with everyone having a great laugh together.*

Finally, reflect on the whole situation, asking yourself what you might do differently if you could do it again: *I think making the 'cheesiness' deliberate allowed the students to feel laughed WITH, rather than laughed AT, giving them control. However, in hindsight, there might have been students who wanted to write more serious poetry who didn't get the opportunity, so perhaps if I were to do it again I'd keep the 'best poem' prize in addition to the 'cheesy' one.*

Using this technique allows you to tell a full story

without rambling on and on. It also lets you comment on your past actions, giving yourself credit where it's due but also criticising yourself when you deserve it. This way, the interviewer will be able to see that you can admit your mistakes, and what you would do in the situation *now*.

WHEN YOU DON'T KNOW

Sometimes, no matter how meticulously you've prepared for your interview, you'll be thrown a question that results in a shrug and a sorry look from your evidently empty brain. This situation is terrifying for absolutely anyone that finds themselves in it. Obviously, we can't magically bestow that knowledge upon you, but what we can do is give you a simple process to approach this situation in the best way possible.

Ask them to repeat/rephrase. It really can be something as simple as hearing the question put in different words that makes it click in your mind and gives you the perfect answer. If not, then you've at least bought yourself a few extra seconds to think about your response.

Admit you don't know. It might be embarrassing to admit that you don't know the answer, but it'll be more embarrassing if you stumble your way through a total guess. Sure, telling the interviewer that you don't know the answer won't look great, but it'll look miles better than pretending you do. As in most places, an honest failure is better than a dishonest success.

Make an educated guess. Say to the interviewer that, although you don't know the answer, you'll try your best to respond to the question. Then, give an answer that is as close to correct as you can manage.

Ask to explain yourself. Ask the interviewer if you can give your reasons for why you gave that answer. Explain that you used certain information that you do know to try to bridge the gap to what you don't.

Ask for feedback. Finally, tell the interviewer that, although you didn't know the answer and tried your best, you would be interested in hearing the correct answer and how close you were to it.

We're not saying that if you use this technique, you'll come out of this situation unscathed; depending on the importance of the question, lacking the knowledge required to answer it may indicate that you don't have the level of experience that the company is looking for. However, for questions with slightly lower stakes, where it is less vital to know the correct answer, this technique will demonstrate your ability to handle pressure, as well as a certain level of maturity by admitting your ignorance and using your logical reasoning skills to figure out some semblance of an answer despite it.

STORYTELLING

This isn't so much its own separate technique as something you should keep in mind throughout the interview. We as people are geared towards stories and narratives. Our brains like it when information is organised into a series of events that has a beginning, middle and an end, and connects with us on some emotional level. You can see this in the common memory technique known as the 'Mental Journey': if you have a list of things to remember, it can be easier to memorise the information by representing each list item with an object that you place in a story. It's much easier to remember the story, and therefore the objects that you interact with in it, than the plain information.

In the same way, your interviewer will be much more engaged if you give your answers in the form of stories (remember, though, to keep them more fact than fiction). Create narratives, victories and defeats, twists and turns, characters, suspense – the more exciting you make your answers, the more excited your interviewer will be about you. Obviously, you should pick your moments, because if you give a lengthy story answer to every question you're asked, the interview will go on for hours, but preparing a couple of stories that you'll be able to whip out at some point is a great way to bring some character to the interview.

   With those techniques covered, you should be able to answer any question sent your way. Now, what could those questions look like?

CHAPTER 7

COMMON QUESTIONS

The questions you'll be asked in the interview can be split into three top-level categories:

1. Do you match this company's goals, values and culture?
2. Do you have the skills and qualities required to perform your role effectively?
3. Do you have goals and ambitions beyond just getting paid?*

Beyond these, there are the hidden meanings behind each question that we discussed earlier. We've split the questions into smaller categories and beneath some placed potential hidden meanings in italics (but remember to consider the hidden meanings

*In fact, even this could be said to come under number 1.

for the others, too). It would be wise to come up with some kind of answer to each of these questions, but remember there will be others more specific to your role.

PERSONAL

- What have you been up to?
  Do you spend your time wisely?
- Tell me about yourself.
- If you were an animal/fictional character/chocolate bar/17th century poet, which would you be?
  How do you see yourself? What qualities do you pride yourself on?
- How would your friends/last boss/family/pets describe you?
  Are you self-aware? How much do you care what others think?
- What is your greatest strength?
- What is your greatest weakness?
  Can you accept and work on your own faults? What should we watch out for?
- What makes you unique?
- Tell me something that isn't on your CV.
- How do you handle success/failure/pressure/stress?
- Do you consider yourself successful? Why?

What's your outlook on life? What do you value?

- Are you nice?

  How much do you value kindness? Do you strike a balance between doormat and downright prat?

- What are your pet peeves?

  How much/easily do you let things bother you?

- What motivates you?

  Do you fit with the way we motivate our staff?

- Are you self-motivated?
- What are you passionate about?
- What are your hobbies?

  Are you an interesting person?

- What are your goals?
- What is your dream job?
- Would you rather be liked or respected?
- What's your greatest achievement?
- If you could go back and re-live the last five/ten years, what would you do differently?

  Do you let your regrets hold you back?

- What's the worst thing you've got away with?

  Are you responsible? Do you bend the rules when you need to?

YOUR LAST JOB

- Why did you leave your last job?
- What won't you miss about your last job?

Are you going to have similar problems here?

- Why do you want to change jobs?
- Why were you let go from your previous position?

  Are you willing to accept responsibility for your mistakes?

- What have you been doing since your last job?
- Why have you been out of work this long?
- What was the biggest criticism you received from your last boss?

  How do you handle criticism? Do you get defensive?

- What was the biggest problem you faced at your last job?
- Why weren't you promoted at your last job?

HOW YOU WORK

- Describe your work ethic.
- In what environment do you work best?
- Do you work well independently/with others?
- Do you take your work home with you?

  Do you manage your time, and balance work and life, effectively?

- How would you describe the pace at which you work?
- What strategies do you use to motivate your team?
- Who was your best/worst boss and why?

  What's the best way to manage you?

- What do you expect from a manager/supervisor?
- If you were 100% sure a manager was wrong about something, how would you handle it? What about 80%?

  What's your relationship to authority? Do you have tact?

- Tell me about a time that your boss was wrong.
- What makes a team work well together?
- Tell me about a time that you had a heavy workload and how you handled it.
- Have you ever had to deal with a problem employee?

  How do you handle conflict?

EXPERIENCE AND QUALIFICATIONS

- What applicable experience do you have?
- What's your opinion of this industry trend/ company?
- Are you overqualified for this position?

  Will you be comfortable here? Is this what you really want?

- What can you do for us better than the other candidates?
- Tell me about your educational background.
- Why are you taking a lower level position than your previous role?

Are you going to leave as soon as something better comes along?

- What's the biggest challenge you've ever had at work?
- What have you learned from your mistakes?

  Do you learn from your mistakes?

- What was your biggest accomplishment/failure at work?
- What's the biggest risk you've taken at work? Did it pay off?

  Do you take risks wisely? Do you only ever play it safe?

- Give an example of a time you demonstrated integrity/showed initiative/thought outside the box/ displayed leadership skills.
- Why should we hire you?
- Why shouldn't we hire you?

  Are you self-aware? Are you persuasive enough to flip this?

- What was your most rewarding job?
- Can you explain this gap in your CV?

THIS ROLE

- What do you know about the company?
- How does this role fit in with your career aspirations?

  Do you have aspirations? Is this just a stepping stone

to you?

- What are your salary expectations/requirements?
- Why do you want to work here?

  Did you apply for this job blindly?

- Would you be willing to relocate?
- Would you be willing to travel?
- When would you be looking to start?
- How would you adjust to working here?
- What will you find least/most challenging about this job?

  What are your strengths/weaknesses?

- What ability/trait/quality of yours will help you best here?
- What can we expect from you in your first 30/60 days?

  Do you think ahead?

- What's your impression of the culture here?
- Is there anything you'd like to know about the company or position that I haven't already told you?
- Do you have any reservations about the job?

  Have you been actively listening? Are you just a 'yes' person?

THE FUTURE

- Where would you like to be in 5/10 years?
- How do you plan to achieve your goals?

Do you actively work towards your goals?

- What are you hoping to achieve while here?
- What is it important for you to have in this job?

  What do we need to do to make you stick around?

- What will you do if you don't get this position?

  Do you plan to reapply later or just move on? How committed are you to working at this company?

CURVEBALLS

Finally, there are the questions like 'Sell me this pen', 'This apple is a bomb; what do you do?', or 'How many window washers are there in London?' These questions are designed to throw you off so that the interviewer can see how you think and how you operate under pressure. The important thing to remember when you are asked one of these questions is that your answer isn't what matters, but how you get there. Don't panic, take your time and ask clarifying questions to define the parameters. If you can demonstrate some out-of-the-box thinking, that's brilliant, but your priority should be to keep calm and work your way through it.

There are hundreds more questions you may get asked in the interview. Almost all of them will simply be a reinterpretation of one of the questions we've listed here, but remember that the purpose of every single question is to answer just one:

Are you who we need?

Of course, your interviewer isn't the only one who'll be asking questions...

CHAPTER 8

GOT ANY QUESTIONS FOR ME?

We've already stressed in this section the importance of asking your interviewer questions. We've also mentioned that when they ask for those questions, 'I think you've already answered them all' is not a great response. That's because this will only be the case if you've just prepared a handful – ideally, your brain should be stacked full of 20, 50, 100 potential questions. You don't have to ask all of them, of course, just the ones that seem the most relevant or are burning the biggest holes in your head.

So, you might wonder what a good question looks like. You'll see plenty of advice online in articles titled something like '8 Great Questions to Ask in Interviews', with examples intended to sound clever and out-of-the-box: 'Where do *you* see yourself in five years?', 'What can I do to sit in your chair as soon as possible?', 'What's your least favourite thing about your job?'

In reality, these aren't the best questions to ask at all, because interviewers can tell that you're just asking them to sound clever and score some points. Remember, they're not idiots; they will probably have seen those lists, too, and will only hear your lack of originality. Truthfully, the best questions you can ask are the ones you are genuinely curious to know the answers to. This is why it's important to have as many questions as possible: if you have no questions, then you clearly aren't that curious about the company. Curiosity is almost a direct synonym of interest, so a lack of curiosity about the role will communicate an equal absence of interest.

That said, we recognise that even if you are interested in a company it can be a little difficult to get the motor running when trying to think of questions. To assist with this, we've prepared a list of questions you can use as a jumping-off point. If you decide to use these questions, try your best to tailor them to the company; while you shouldn't ask questions purely to show off the research you've done, personalising a question to a company does demonstrate a certain level of care and attention.

QUESTIONS YOU COULD ASK

- I know the larger responsibilities of the role, but what are some of the smaller tasks I'll be performing day-to-day?
- What are some of the most vital qualities a person needs to excel in this role?
- What would your expectations of me be over the first 30 days/six months/year?
- What do you like or dislike about the culture here?
- Where do you see the company headed over the next five years?
- Who do you consider your fiercest competitor?
- What are the biggest opportunities/challenges facing the company/department at the moment?
- What has been the typical career path for people in this role?
- What are the next steps in the interview process?
- Aside from the obvious, what are the biggest perks/benefits of working in this role?
- How has the company changed/adapted over the last few years?
- Are there any programmes in place for new employees to enter the company smoothly?
- What additional opportunities or duties might I have here?

- What projects would I begin on?
- Is this a new role or am I replacing someone else? If so, what sort of shoes will I be trying to fill?
- Are this role's responsibilities more fixed or fluid?
- How will I be trained?
- What programmes do you have in place for professional development?
- How will my performance be measured and assessed?
- How long have you been with the company?
- Has your role changed much in the time you've been here?
- I've read what it says about the company on the website, but can you tell me more about [...]?
- What are the company's current goals? Are you on track to achieve them?
- Can you tell me more about the team I'll be working with?
- Who will I be working with most closely?
- Could you tell me about the person I'll report to?
- What are the team's biggest strengths or weaknesses?
- Should I know about any topics that my team members are sensitive about?
- Are you expecting to make any more hires in this department in the next six months?
- Could you tell me about the last team event you held?

- What's your favourite office tradition?
- Do any of the team spend time together outside work?
- Do you ever hold joint events or competitions with other companies/departments?
- What have you found to be unique about this company as opposed to other places you've worked?
- Do you have any concerns about me or my background?
- Is there anything else you'd like to know about me, or anything I could provide you with?

Remember that these questions are all quite surface level; it's best to ask questions specific to the company or industry, and there's no substitute for genuine curiosity.

CHAPTER 9

AFTER THE INTERVIEW

A wave of relief may rush over you when the interviewer slaps their knees and says 'Well, I think that's everything!' That's natural, and you should let yourself bathe in that wave. However, you also need to remember that although the last question has been asked, the interview is not necessarily over.

Your first thought should be about next steps. If you don't know what to expect over the next few days – whether you'll be told your progress either way, whether you'll be required to fill out any forms, how many stages still stand between you and the job – it is imperative that you ask. Many candidates feel inexplicably awkward about this, but interviewers don't want to keep you in the dark. They won't give you any cryptic Gandalf-like instructions to *look to my coming at first light on the fifth day*. They will probably just tell you to wait for an email or phone call in a couple of days.

After this is clarified, feel free to have a more casual conversation with your interviewer (as for just *how* casual, always take the interviewer's lead). It will almost always be acceptable to ask how the rest of their day looks or, if the interview took place at the end of the day, how it had gone up until the interview. Generally, you don't want to be walked out of the building in awkward, polite silence. If the conversation becomes quite familiar in tone, be careful that your post-interview relief doesn't loosen your tongue to the point of 'incriminating' yourself – don't accidentally tell them that you lied in or made up your answers, or speak too openly about the less *professional* aspects of your personal life; remember that whatever you say may still be used against you.

However well the interview went, whether the interviewer is your new best friend or you accidentally insulted their family, you must *always* end with a handshake and a thank you. Not only is this polite, it's wise: you never know what the future holds. This interview may have gone terribly, but perhaps your good attitude will put you in good stead for a role you may interview for later. Or perhaps the interview didn't go quite as badly as you'd thought, and it's your *lack* of a thank you that pushes the interviewer to decide not to invite you back. It's always far safer (not to mention nicer) to extend your gratitude for the opportunity.

When you get home, or on your journey back, draw up some notes on how the interview went. Jot down what went well, what could have gone better, and what you need to do to perform better at your next interview. You should also detail the next steps so that you know what to expect. If you do this for every interview you have, not only will it help you to keep track of where you are in each process, it'll give you a great picture of your strengths and weaknesses. It'll also reduce the risk of mixing up your research on one company with research on another, preventing some embarrassing situations in interviews.

If you have trouble organising notes, we really recommend a free online tool called **Trello**. It's used by many businesses (including ours) for project management, but it's also a great way for individuals to organise themselves. Within it you can incorporate goals, checklists, deadlines, images and attachments, with everything being incredibly user-friendly. Give it a go if you often find yourself scrolling through pages of title-less notes in your phone, trying to find the two lines you wrote about that one idea you had three months ago.

CHAPTER 10

CONCLUSION

You should now be prepared to enter any interview with the confidence to sail through it. Before we move on to Section 5, however, we want to reiterate and stress a couple of things:

Firstly, 90% of your success in an interview is down to how well you prepare for it. Think of it like an exam: you get asked questions, and you're judged on how well you answer them. You wouldn't stroll into an exam without studying, would you? It's the same here, in that the better you prepare, the better the interview will go.

That said, the second thing we want to reiterate is that while you should absolutely prepare, do not over-rehearse all of your answers. If you do, you'll risk sounding robotic and inauthentic.

Thirdly, remember to be friendly and engaging to everyone you meet. We don't mean this to say we assume you'd scowl at the cleaning staff, but often when we're nervous we'll become self-absorbed and barely make eye contact with the receptionist, let alone smile at them and strike up a conversation. There are two problems with this: the interviewer may well ask them for their impression of you and your demeanour, and you'll have missed an opportunity to soothe your nerves by having a casual conversation with someone.

Something we haven't talked about very much is body language. We didn't want to make too big a deal of it, because while there is some truth in the theory of 'power poses' and the like, a person trying too hard to pull this off will inevitably shoot themselves in the foot with the obviousness of it, rendering the whole thing counterproductive. We did want to mention it, however, as you should be aware of the energy that you give off with your body language. You don't want to close yourself off with crossed arms, staring at the floor – this communicates a lack of confidence and, sometimes, the notion that you're hiding something. Nor do you want to pop your feet up on the desk and open your shirt down to the third button, for reasons we hope are obvious. All in all, you should be self-aware, but not self-conscious.

Finally, we spoke earlier about being friendly to

everyone, and, at the risk of sounding cheesy, we include yourself within that. We say this because many people develop a self-deprecating sense of humour as part of their personality. While we aren't here to give you mindfulness or self-help advice, self-deprecation is an absolute interview-killer. Even if it's intended as a joke, if you imply you're a bad or incompetent person in any way, the interviewer is likely to go ahead and believe you. It can be tempting, especially if you've developed a habit of breaking awkward social tension with it, but we urge you to leave that mentality at home. Similarly, if you don't make it to the next stage of the interview, do your best not to take it personally. Not being a match for a company professionally is like not being a match for a person romantically: it doesn't mean you're a terrible person, just that they aren't right for you. All you have to do is trust that you'll find your corporate soulmate eventually, perhaps with a couple of enjoyable bad decisions along the way.

That's it! If you've read through all the previous sections, you should be prepared for every aspect of the job search process right up until you get the offer. But what comes after? How do you slot smoothly into that new role once you've snagged it? Well, that's what Section 5: **Beginning Your New Job** is for.

SECTION FIVE

BEGINNING YOUR NEW JOB

CHAPTER 1

YOU'RE NOT QUITE DONE YET

Look, we're not trying to harsh anyone's mellow. You've just landed your new job and, yes, you absolutely should celebrate! Go out, have a few too many drinks and dance the night away.

In the haze of your hangover, however, you might recognise a faint spectre of anxious terror. Where could this be coming from? You've already completed all the interviews, and you have the offer secured. That's it, right? Unfortunately, like many newlyweds discovering that a wedding is followed by a marriage, job-seekers might be slow to grasp that a job offer is followed by a job. In fact, this is a surprisingly apt metaphor, so forgive us if we indulge in it for a moment.

You've spent years waiting for this moment. So much time wasted hopping from partner to partner, each with their various virtues and vices, each eventually proving not to be worth the effort. You are somewhat ashamed to admit that, from time to time, there has been something of an *overlap* between one and another – you weren't sure you'd be able to function without *someone*, and you *certainly* weren't about to move back in with Mum and Dad.

But, after all the heartbreak, you've found the one. They've got everything you could ever hope for, and they're a match for you in every way. They even seem as excited about you as you are about them! You speed through the courting process, and, before you know it, they've proposed! You accept, of course, partly because they're your dream partner and partly because you've been subsisting exclusively on ramen noodles for the past three months. So you make it official. You do all the paperwork, you move in and you both start your life together.

It goes great ... for a while. Pretty soon, however, they begin blindsiding you with work you did not expect to have to do. Suddenly, you're doing the dishes, scrubbing tiles and removing weeds in the garden. You try to complain, but they point out that this is all pretty standard stuff that has to be done, and if it has to be done by *someone*, why not you? Despite this sound logic, you start to resent your new partner; you thought you'd just be doing all the nice stuff, the stuff you thought you'd signed up for. You didn't think it would come with all this *busy work.*

This unabashed grumpiness clouds your judgement, masking all your partner's pros and causing you only to see the cons. Soon enough, you're eyeing up other people on the street, looking up the names of divorce lawyers and drafting a goodbye Post-it note.

Simultaneously, your partner has noticed that you're not doing your share, that they're having to pick up your slack and that your heart just doesn't seem to be in it. Before you even have a chance to announce that you're leaving, they tell you to get out. Just like that, you've thrown away the best partner you've ever had, all because you weren't prepared to do the small amount of unwanted work required to keep them.

It's a pretty bleak view, we know. This is, however, the reality for many a jobseeker who expected only to do the top three things listed in the job description. This is especially true for creative, artistic jobs. The famous saying is that if you find a job you love, you'll never have to work a day in your life. Unfortunately, this is painfully untrue: movie stars still have to learn lines and even astronauts have to do paperwork. Just as with a romantic relationship, if you expect that loving a job will make everything about it easy, the shock of discovering a small amount of difficulty might lead you mistakenly to believe you don't love it all that much after all. If, instead, you prepare for and expect at least *some* difficulty now and then, you might be pleasantly surprised by how little there is.

So you might be wondering how you might go about preparing for your new job. Let us help you out.

CHAPTER 2

LEAVING YOUR OLD JOB

If you're leaving one job for another, now is the time to resign. This can be a stressful and messy process – it requires tact, empathy and maturity. Sure, it can be tempting to stick up both middle fingers and stroll backwards out of your boss's office, listing all the objects they can insert into various places and the misfortunes you hope to befall them in the near future, but the irritating truth is that it's unwise to burn those bridges; no matter how pleasant the initial heat feels on your face, pretty soon you'll be left with nothing but ash, charcoal and the realisation that you may have left some important stuff on the other side of the river. Wading through rushing water that could have been left under the bridge can be dangerous, and you don't want to turn up to your new work with soggy shoes. With that in mind, we'll begin with some advice on how to transition from your job a little more gracefully.

YOUR LETTER OF RESIGNATION

Your first challenge is to tell your boss that you're leaving. Whether your relationship with them is a positive or negative one, it can be difficult not to let your feelings influence the language of the letter. It is best, however, to keep this document as professional as possible; anything you'd like to say on a sentimental or emotional level can be said in a separate email.

For the beginning, all you need to do is formally acknowledge that this document is a notice of resignation from your current position, and the date from which it will be effective. Here, you *must* pay attention to your position's contracted notice period, and give at least that whole period. You can give more if you like, but never less: if your contracted notice period is two weeks, don't say your resignation will be effective as of next Tuesday.* It might look something like this:

---

*There is a chance that your boss will relieve you of your duties before your time is up, but don't expect this – plan to work the entire period.

To [Boss's Name],

Please accept this letter as formal notification that I will be resigning from my position as [your position] with [company]. My final day will be [your last day].

Technically, this is all you really need, as it contains all the information you have to convey. However, it's worth including the following things in addition to this in order to make the transition easier for everyone and to preserve relations in case you require a reference in the future (or, in the worst case scenario, your new job doesn't work out and you need to ask for your old one back).

Next, thank your employer for the opportunity they've given you and the experience you've acquired through your work. Consider listing some of your favourite projects and responsibilities and the important things you've learned in your time there. Feel free to be a little sentimental here, but keep the tone ultimately professional.

Finally, communicate your willingness to assist in the handover of your responsibilities to other staff, whether that be by training someone new or spreading those duties among the current team. You don't need to go into great detail, just let them know that you intend to make your departure as smooth as possible for everyone involved. This will probably come as a great relief to your boss, who likely has enough on their plate already without losing one of their staff members. You could say:

During my final [notice period], I'll do everything possible to wrap up my duties and train other team members. Please let me know if there's anything else I can do to help during the transition.

After that, all that's left to do is to wrap up and sign off the letter in a way that lets your boss know that you bear no ill will towards them or the company (even if it may not be the case, it's wise to keep the door open):

I wish you and the company continued success, and I hope to stay in touch in the future.

Kind regards,

[Your name and signature]

Once you have your letter written, you have the choice of how to deliver it. If you know that your boss is a busy person who may be likely to miss/ignore an email, a signed physical letter left on their desk not only ensures that they will see it, but it also adds a touch of class. If you fear that they will deliberately ignore your letter for the purposes of claiming never to have received it, thus delaying the beginning of the notice period, physically handing them the letter and informing them of its contents before walking away is a sometimes necessary, if quite cold, move. Either way, asking for some form of acknowledgement from your employer is always a good idea, as it prevents a situation where you walk out of the office on your final day only to receive a text from your now ex-boss saying, 'So on Monday I need you to ...'

Your boss may respond in one of a few different ways. The ideal response, of course, is to accept your resignation with a combination of sadness and support: sorry to see you go but excited to see what you achieve next. Unfortunately, it won't always be like this. Undesirable reactions range on a spectrum from apathy to outright refusal. In the case of the latter, don't be afraid. Once your boss has acknowledged your notice (and, yes, a refusal is an acknowledgement), the notice period has begun. They have no power to hold you in a job longer than the time you are contractually obligated. If they try to force you to stay, put your foot down and state in a calm, professional manner that you appreciate the inconvenience you may be causing them, but that this move is vital for your professional development (and, if you can't help but inject a little venom, your mental well-being). Keep in mind that nothing they say can force you to stay.

COUNTER OFFERS

Your boss may offer you more money, more responsibilities or any number of things to get you to stay. Be wary of these offers. They can often be tempting, but remember that you are probably leaving for more than just money. For whatever counter offer you may receive, ask yourself if what has been offered will *solve* the problems you have with the company, or simply *mask* them – there's only so much Febreze you can spray before you're better off leaving the bathroom.

On the off chance that it really is just more money you were after, it's still worth asking if your problem was that you simply weren't paid enough, or rather that the company didn't *value* you enough. If this is the case, consider that their offer to pay you more only when you decided to leave reveals that they knew your value all along and *deliberately* paid you less than you were worth. To return to our relationship analogy, if you have to threaten your partner with divorce for them to show you the appreciation you deserve, is that really a relationship in which you wish to stay?

You might also feel the urge to game the system by going to your new employer and informing them of the counter-offer. Your gamble may well pay off, and they may offer you more money in order to get you to choose them. Conversely, they might decide that your hesitation is a sign that you are not as committed to their company as they'd hoped, and wish you luck in the future. In this situation, it's worth remembering that you had already accepted an offer. Don't get greedy.

TELLING EVERYONE ELSE

It is worth noting that your boss must always be the first to know, even if you are dying to tell your best work friend. The reason for this is that standard rumour rules apply when leaving a job: you only tell the people you *really* trust, instructing them not to tell anyone; they agree, and so only tell the people they *really* trust; and so on. Only so many iterations can occur before someone *really* trusts your boss. Mark Twain supposedly once said, 'Two men can keep a secret if one of them is dead.' Of course, we would now also include women and non-binary people in that, but there is an element of truth to it.

Once your boss does know (and you've received acknowledgment to that effect), it's time to let everyone else know, too. This step is really up to you. In fact, you could choose not to tell anyone at all if you'd like the drama of having your continued absence gradually noticed by everyone until the penny eventually drops. If, however, this option is impractical due to being required to train someone new or for some other reason, then you may have to come up with a way to communicate your departure. You might want to send an email, cc'ing everyone in your team, informing them of your decision and thanking them for their support and friendship (if any has been given) over your time there.

If there are a couple of colleagues with whom you have a closer relationship, who might feel that such an email would be a little impersonal, consider sending a more personal one to them first. You could even be a little more sentimental and give them a handwritten card. You might want to arrange a final lunch or pub trip with your team to say goodbye, if that matches the culture. You may even find that something will be arranged for you, depending on how long you've been with the company. We would always recommend participating fully with these events – even if you weren't very happy at your job, you can at least make the last memory a good one.

DURING THE NOTICE PERIOD

It is deceptively easy to become complacent during your final weeks, especially if your workload is gradually easing as it's handed over to other people. However, having one of the team leave is something that will cause stress and inconvenience for everyone else, so a willingness to lend a helping hand in making sure the transition is seamless will be greatly appreciated, and will solidify you as a positive figure in the minds of the team. Keep turning up on time, finish the work you've been given and try your best not to make this time any more difficult for the others.

YOUR LAST DAY

It's time to tie up all your loose ends. This refers to work, of course, in the sense that you should check with your boss or any colleagues to see if there's anything they need before you leave, but it also refers to your personal life: if you have any love to declare for the office temp with whom you've been subtly flirting for the past six months, speak now or forever hold your peace.

Make sure you haven't left anything in the building – you don't want to make a dramatic exit only to come slinking back in to pick up the phone charger you keep in your third desk drawer. If you need to, write a list during the notice period of everything you have in the building. Anything you *don't* think of during that time can't really be that important, anyway.

Finally, make sure that you have the contact information of anyone you want to keep in touch with. Regardless of your personal relationships, it's wise to remain networked with the key players in the company from a professional perspective.

At the end of the day, stroll out of the building with your head held high, safe in the knowledge that you're taking a step forward in your career ... and your life.

CHAPTER 3

BEFORE YOU START

There are a few things you ought to do before your first day to ensure you can glide into the office fully prepared.

First, make sure that any paperwork, whether physical or digital, is completed as quickly as possible. This will show good faith and will save your new employer some stress: if they send you some forms to fill out and receive nothing but 48 hours of radio silence in return, they might start to panic and think that you've decided you're not interested in the job after all. In addition to forms, there might be onboarding documentation, such as an employee handbook to read, so that you can familiarise yourself with company policy. Getting it all done in a timely manner will set a tone of enthusiasm and competency, which are the two most desirable traits in a new employee.

Keep in touch with your new employer, and check with them to see if they need anything from you before or on your first day, whether it's identification, information or equipment (ask them whether you'll be provided with any technology or if you'll be expected to bring your own). You should also use this time to flag up any holidays you have booked or ask any pertinent unanswered questions about dress code, scheduling, company culture or any other logistical issues that may not have come up in your interviews. You might even ask if there are any books or articles you could read that would help you with the role. Obviously, you shouldn't pester your new boss with an unending stream of emails, but a healthy amount of curiosity about your new position will display a certain level of excitement.

If you happen to have a period of free time before your new job, *take advantage of it*. Being in the middle of a job search can cause you to feel guilty about doing anything else – you can't relax without thinking you should probably be looking at job boards, polishing your CV or typing up a cover letter. Now that you have that job waiting, you can fill the remaining time with whatever you wish. For example, you could take this opportunity to do all those odd jobs around the house that you never had the chance to get around to: you don't want to walk into the living room in a month's time and remember that you were intending to repaint it at some point. That said, if you'd rather swaddle yourself in a blanket cocoon, surrounded by snacks, and watch movies for the better part of a week, then go ahead: you've earned it. The only caveat we'd offer is that, if your job has involved a relocation, it is vital you get your new home sorted first: it's very easy to procrastinate and say that you can do it all on evenings and weekends, but if you're putting it off when you have free time, how do you think you'll feel after a whole day/week of work?

Get on LinkedIn and put everything in order. This means changing your status so that you're no longer looking for a job, following your new company's up-dates and stalking your new colleagues, connecting with as many in your team as you can find; it will be much easier to strike up a conversation with some-one if you know each other's face, and if you can find something you have in common. You should also have a quick look at the rest of your social media to ensure that there's nothing you wouldn't want a new colleague to find.

Practise your morning commute, at whatever time you'd need to make it. It might be a bit of a bore to get up early without needing to, but it means there will be one less stressful variable to deal with on your first day. You can also use the opportunity to explore the area and locate some good places to get food, drinks and groceries, as well as possible destinations for after-work gatherings.

If you have the means, go out and treat yourself! Securing a new job is one event in life that is categorically worth celebrating, and we'd suggest doing so with a couple of new outfits you can wear to work, and some new stationery. You'd be surprised how big an effect a new wardrobe and notebook can have on your mindset – it can really cement the idea that this is a new chapter in your life.

Speaking of mindset, it might sound wishy-washy, but we really recommend building yourself a goal board. This can take whatever form you want, whether it's something physical like a white/chalk/corkboard, a collection of fridge magnets or a set of Post-it notes on your bedroom door, or a collage of images set as your desktop background. We say this because reaching your new job can feel like you've crested the peak of a mountain: it's an incredible feeling that lasts all of five minutes before you realise the only way is down. Once you've been working for a few weeks, you may feel like you're stuck and no longer moving forward. It's important to keep setting achievable, realistic goals for yourself that you can quantifiably work towards so that you can keep adding subsequent peaks to the mountain and continue climbing up it. You do this because the peaks are not the source of happiness in and of themselves: it's *approaching* the peaks that makes us happy. This is also why it's important not to place the peaks too far out of reach, because feeling that they're too far away can be worse than not having them there at all. And, of course, you should add the job search to the goal board simply so that you can make it the first item you cross off the list. We'll talk more about goals later, but, for now, we'll move on to your first day.

CHAPTER 4

DAY 1

So the big day has arrived and there's a chance you'll be feeling like a child on the first day of school, experiencing a combination of excitement, nerves and a twinge of sadness that you can no longer lounge around the house in your pyjamas watching cartoons. It can be stressful running through a mental checklist to see if you've got everything you need to bring with you and have done everything you need to do. One way to reduce this stress is to move that checklist from mental to physical. Here's a good baseline:

✓ Wake up earlier than you need to – set multiple alarms if you know you're a heavy sleeper.
✓ Dress well – adhere to whatever dress code given, but don't agonise over your outfit too much.

✓ Bring a water bottle – while it's true that there'll undoubtedly be water there, it'll be worth bringing one with you to drink on the commute and to refill as a way of being environmentally conscious.

✓ Budget for lunch out instead of bringing it with you if you can – asking co-workers out for lunch on your first day is a great way to bond.

✓ If you do pack a lunch, avoid packing anything messy or nasally offensive – you don't want people's impression of you marred by your garlic breath.

✓ Bring any identification you've been asked for – this might be your driving licence, passport or a photo for your ID badge.

✓ Just for today, make your commute half an hour earlier than you need to – today's the day you're most likely to be late and the most important day to be on time.

✓ When you get to the office, be professional and greet everyone you see – you don't need to go around shaking the hand of every bystander, but a small smile goes a long way.

✓ Turn off your phone and any smart tech – it's better to be told you can turn them on than be told you should have turned them off.

✓ Become a sponge – soak up as much information as you can, writing down anything that might fall through the cracks.

✓ Put extra effort in to make a good impression, but

don't over-commit yourself – you don't know how much time and effort this job will take yet, so you don't want to over-encumber yourself.

✓ Ask for help – no one expects you to know exactly what you're doing from the get-go. In fact, asking questions shows interest and enthusiasm (just make sure to listen properly to the answers).

✓ Don't be afraid to answer questions, even if you're unsure of your response – a willingness to fail is better than a refusal to try.

✓ Be flexible – you may be used to a certain way of doing things thanks to your old place of work, but you're going to need to compromise with the way they're done here (at least for now: you can always suggest changes later).

✓ Take note of the metrics by which your success will be measured – it could be certain targets, quotas, or periodic review meetings.

✓ Confirm with your colleagues, especially your boss, how they prefer to communicate, both casually and when you need to reach them directly – do they prefer to keep all work communications through email? Do they use WhatsApp? Do they prefer a phone call?

✓ Stay late to take notes on what you did well and on what you need to improve – if your new boss specifically tells you to go home early, however, go ahead.

It's most important just to get through the day with a positive, optimistic outlook: things can and will go wrong on your first day – it's what first days are for – but it will make a huge difference if you can roll with the punches with a smile on your face.

CHAPTER 5

CONVERSATION STARTERS

We realise that it may feel childish to concern your-self with making new friends at work (*What if they make fun of my shoes?*), but the reality is that the people who surround you make a monumental difference to your happiness. For this reason, we think it's not only perfectly natural, but entirely wise, to spend some time thinking about how you're going to interact with your new colleagues. As with all social situations, there's a delicate balance involved: you don't want to come across too forward, nor do you want to ignore everyone and end up blending into the wallpaper.

We've taken the liberty of drawing up a list of questions that you can use to strike up a conversation. While it's always better to weigh in on an ongoing conversation, feel free to lean on this list when you need to. Just don't fire them all off at once.

AT WORK

- Who's the most influential person you've learned from here, and why?
- How long have you been here? How long have you been in this role?
- What are you working on at the moment?
- Do you have any advice for a new starter?
- What would you do differently if you started here again?
- Do you know any books or videos that might help me here?
- What does success in business mean to you?
- Is there anything I should steer clear of?
- What team do you work in? Who works in it with you?
- Where's the best place to get some food around here?
- Have you read any good books recently?
- How was your commute today?
- What's the best/worst project you've ever worked on?
- Have you attended any cool company/industry events?

AT LUNCH

- If you could eat only one type of food for the rest of your life, what would it be, and why?
- What's the weirdest food combination you've ever tried?
- What's your idea of the perfect day?
- What's your idea of the perfect lunch?
- What's the best/worst restaurant you've ever been to?
- What's your favourite comfort food?
- What's your favourite comfort TV show/movie?
- If you could live anywhere in the world, where would it be?
- Where's the most exotic place you've ever been?
- What music do you listen to that I wouldn't expect?

WHILE NETWORKING

- What's the worst present you've ever received and why?
- Who's your favourite comedian?
- What are the top three items on your bucket list?
- What's the biggest risk you've ever taken?
- Do you have any phobias?
- If you could have dinner with anyone living or dead, who would it be?

- Are you a cat person or a dog person?
- What would be your superpower of choice?
- If you won the lottery, what would be your first splurge?
- What's your favourite fact?
- What's your favourite joke?
- What's the most interesting thing about your hobby?
- Got any fun plans for the weekend?

While you shouldn't prepare an answer to every one of these questions yourself, you should definitely be ready to be asked 'So, tell me about yourself!' Much too often the answer to this will consist of a long pause, an 'er ...', a shrug and an 'I dunno, really'. We're not saying you should prepare a speech or write a script, but just think about some key information – your hometown, where you went to school/university, your hobbies, what sort of music you're into, your family, any major events that shaped your life, anything that might help someone get to know you. That said, don't alienate them by delving far too deep into your personal traumas.

As we said before, the people you work with have a huge effect on your happiness. However, we do want to state for the record that this doesn't mean they *determine* your happiness – ultimately, that's down to you. There is a chance that, when you get to work, you'll be met by a bunch of people who would rather keep their heads down and their eyes on the job, rather than make any new friends. This may well be exactly how you feel, too; in which case, hooray! If not, however, don't despair. For one thing, you'll likely make at least one friend after some time there, and often it's these rare friends that become the closest. It might even be just a matter of slotting into the culture: you might discover that once you find the rhythm of the business, everyone will start to open up. That, or they might save all their friendliness for after-work drinks, where they become a pack of party animals.

Our point is this: don't let it get you down if your place of work is more like the UK version of *The Office* than the US one (even David Brent has his good moments).

CHAPTER 6

30/60/90

Earlier in this section, we spoke about the importance of continuing to set goals after starting your job. These, of course, don't all have to be work-related: they could be about buying a house, learning a skill or a language or reaching general milestones in your life. In this chapter, we want to introduce you to a particular way of structuring your work-related goals to allow for both short and long-term targets.

The method is known as 30/60/90 because it refers to the number of days that pass before you want to reach certain goals. You might have to spend a few days in your role before you understand what is expected of you and what you can expect of yourself, but, once you feel settled, it's a good idea to get this built as soon as possible, because it's an excellent way to prioritise the right things at the right time.

HOW IT WORKS

As the name suggests, there are three sections: one for the first 30 days of your new job, another for the first 60, and a third for the first 90. For each section, you need to think of a goal that you want to have achieved by the time that number of days is up. You're going to split this goal up into a more actionable plan, so don't worry if it's a little general. That said, try your best to keep it to the **SMART** structure:

SPECIFIC – you need to be able to say categorically whether or not this has been achieved. *Be better at my job* won't work as you will definitely be at least a little better at your job by the end of the month. You'll know your goal is specific enough when it is:

MEASURABLE – in order to know whether or not you've achieved your goal (or how close you were if you didn't), you'll need a way to measure your progress and success.

ACHIEVABLE – you may have heard of the powers of manifesting your goals, and that the mere act of writing them down makes them far easier to achieve. While there is a lot of truth to this, simply writing

Become the president of the United States on a white-board won't make it possible if you're not a US citizen, *especially* if it's not even an election year. Writing down goals that are totally outside the realms of possibility will do nothing but take up space.

REALISTIC – this is similar to 'Achievable', but it goes a little further. It can be quite hard to judge, but you need to ensure you're not setting the bar too high for yourself. By all means, challenge yourself, but if you set yourself a goal that is way too far out of reach, you'll end up feeling like a failure even if, by any normal standards, you're actually doing very well.

TRIGGERED – this is less to do with the goal itself, but relates to the actions you take towards that goal. If, for example, your goal is to become an expert in digital marketing, you need to tie the steps you take towards that goal to certain events in the day/week, such as reading marketing books on your journey home, or watching videos before you go to bed. Doing this means that you aren't relying on the fickle and flippant nature of motivation, instead cementing these actions to the much more reliable base of habit.

Once you have your goals for each section sorted, it's time to break them down into a plan. The plan is a step-by-step process that will lead you along the path to the goal. Doing this will allow you to track your progress and give you a better sense of what work needs to be done in order to achieve your goal. Finally, you need to break down the plan into individual actions and update them each time you complete a step. To return to an earlier metaphor, if you think about the goal as a mountain, the plan can be thought of as the smaller peaks leading up to the summit. The action points then become the little flags that lead the way. Suddenly, you don't have to worry about climbing the mountain – just keep moving from flag to flag and you'll get there. The smaller the action points of your goal, the easier it is to act on them, and the more achievable your goal becomes.

You can set as many or as few goals as you want, but we'd advise you to think about it wisely. On the one hand, setting a lot of goals gives you a greater challenge and, therefore, a greater payoff once you achieve them. On the other, keeping track of the action points of so many goals might be confusing and may result in the whole thing tumbling down. The remedy we'd suggest for this would be to separate goals into distinct categories, and have just one per category per month. These categories could include 'Learning', focusing on educating yourself about the company and your role; 'Social', prioritising network-ing and making friends; 'Performance', centred on how well you do your job; or 'Contribution', thinking about how you can make yourself valuable to the company through more than just your role, such as suggesting new ideas or helping people out with problems in their own work. Separating your goals into categories will allow you to compartmentalise and avoid mixing them up with each other.

Finally, remember that the three sections are allowed to overlap – so you can absolutely take steps towards your 60 or 90-day goal in the first 30 days – but they don't have to. In fact, you might make some of your 60 or 90-day goals continuations of your 30-day ones.

EXAMPLE

What follows is an example of one goal for one month. Feel free to play with the structure as much as you feel suits you – after all, no one is going to be checking up on you to make sure you're doing it all 'correctly'.

CATEGORY: Learning

GOAL: Understand all the responsibilities of my job

THE PLAN:
1. Listen during onboarding to what is expected of me and take notes.
2. Write down the main points and get them signed off by my manager to ensure we're in agreement.

3. Learn about the systems we use.
4. Cross-reference the job specification with the components of the job I've been told to work on.
5. Write down questions any time I don't understand something.
6. Ask my manager the non-immediate questions at the start of each day.
7. Set a meeting with my manager at the end of the month to assess my understanding of the role.

CURRENT ACTION POINTS - STEP 1:

- Confirm onboarding meeting with manager
- Set aside a notebook and pen
- Read the job specification

As we said before, doing this allows you to detail your path up the mountain to your goal, rather than standing at the base, looking up at the snow-covered, cloud-masked peak and wondering how you'll ever reach the summit.

CHAPTER 7

CONCLUSION

At the beginning of this section, we used the metaphor of a new marriage to describe starting a new job. We want to close with a different metaphor.

Beginning a new job is like walking through a misty field – you don't really know where you are or where you're going. You can't see more than five feet in front of you, which is scary and confusing. Every now and then, a hand will appear out of the mist holding a spade, a rake, a lawnmower or one of any number of tools, and point somewhere. So – you try your best to stumble over to where you're pretty sure the hand was pointing and start digging/raking/mowing; you're not entirely sure how important the hand was, or how much authority it had to ask you to do anything, and you're not even sure how much time you're supposed to spend enacting its will or why this particular patch of land needed digging, raking or mowing in the first place. In fact, every now and then you find yourself digging up a patch that you could swear you only mowed yesterday. You decide just to keep going until another hand appears, which, of course, it soon does.

After some time and a few misplaced digs, you begin to notice that you can now see for about 10 feet. This extra visibility allows you to notice patterns, and it's not long before you're correctly predicting what tool will come next and where the hand will point. At 20 feet, you're even able to correct a hand when it points to the wrong patch, and you've noticed that the rake-holding hand belongs to a raker who's really just trying to pass their own work on to you, so you give it less priority.

Eventually, you notice that, at some point, the mist retreated to the edges of your field. It's by no means gone, of course – the fog past the fence is practically impenetrable – but you can see all of your patches pretty clearly. The hands may still pass you an un-expected tool every now and then, but they haven't had to point in a very long time. In fact, you've even requested a different tool on one or two occasions, knowing it would better suit the purpose for that par-ticular patch.

This is how any new job will feel. The only differences,

really, are how familiar you may already be with the tools, and the rate at which the mist retreats. Rest assured, though, that while there will always be mist, it will only be a matter of time before it clears. In the meantime, just try your best not to dig up the wrong spot.

CONCLUSION

Here we are at the end of the road. If you've reached this point, you're either completely prepared for your job search or you're one of those odd people who like to read the end of a book before the beginning (even more odd if it's non-fiction). We'll assume you're of the former and say congratulations! By now, we hope you've gained some insights from each of the five sections and are feeling much more confident about your job search than you may have been when you picked this book up. Like we said in the introduction, we doubt you found anything drastically revolutionary in these 230-odd pages. But, if you take all the nuggets of advice that we've offered, we guarantee that you will be miles ahead of the competition.

There is one final element to the job search that we've neglected to mention in this book. We don't like talking about it because, quite honestly, we don't like to acknowledge it as a factor. It's far from the most important ingredient, but we'd be lying if we said it wasn't influential. The factor is this:

Luck.

Yes, unfortunately, there is a certain chunk of luck involved in snagging that job, whether it's the luck of your application happening to be the most recent when the recruiter logged on, or the luck that there was another train you were able to catch to your interview after the first was delayed, or the luck that your interviewer was also a massive fan of *Avatar: The Last Airbender*, so the two of you could bond over Zuko's character arc. Whatever it is, the truth is that there are some parts of the job search journey that may not be under your control. We have two things to say about this.

The first is that, while you can't *perfect* your own luck, you can certainly *improve* it. You can fine-tune your LinkedIn profile so that it appears higher on searches, you can plan your travel to expect the unexpected, and you can research your interviewer to see what they'd like to talk about. Control what you can, and prepare for what you can't.

The second is that what may look like bad luck actually can be good luck in an ugly hat. To illustrate what we mean, we'll tell you a story about an interview Huw went on in November 2019. Having decided that he would leave his last job at Christmas, Huw went to his first interview at a high-profile recruitment agency. He'd already had phone and video interviews, which had both gone as well as he could have hoped. During the in-person interview, however, he was asked for his biggest weakness. Considering all he knows now, it's a little shocking that he hadn't prepared for this. Huw's answer, to the best of his memory, went something like this:

Well, er, you know those people who are simultaneously really smart and really stupid? Yeah, that's me.

As if that wasn't bad enough, he was even less prepared for the follow-up question, 'In what way are you really stupid?'

After a few moments of panicked thought, Huw said:

Well, saying something like that in an interview isn't very smart.

It will come as no surprise that Huw did not get the job. That experience, however, forced him to prepare for his interviews better. A couple of months later, Huw was sitting opposite a new interviewer: Matt. Needless to say, that interview went much better. Quite soon into his new job, Huw told Matt about the other interview he'd been on. Matt knew the company, and told Huw that he'd dodged a bit of a bullet: there was no way he would have been happy in that role. Had he given a better answer, he may have been hired, but he would have missed out on a job that was much more suited to him, and this book never would have existed.

In the same way, every time you experience some bad luck in your own job search, consider the possibility that, some time in the future, you'll look back and be grateful for it.

With that, we've said all we need to say. We wish you the best of luck in your job search, whether you're looking right now or just thinking about a change of scenery.

And, if you're a member of the fourth group we mentioned at the start of this book, we hope you find a way off your island before you decide to use this book as kindling.

ABOUT
THE AUTHORS

MATT SEDGWICK

Matt is a talent acquisition specialist with over 10 years of experience in recruitment successfully owning and running two businesses during that time. In his spare time, he enjoys completing construction projects and playing with Pablo the pug.

HUW LANDAUER

Huw began working with Matt as a marketeer after graduating from Queen Mary University of London. He likes to branch out into the arts, writing short stories and, right now, a novel, and creating geometric paintings.